Alphabet logo

Counter-Print Books

In the world of visual identity, the alphabet is more than just a set of characters, it's a universal design language, rich with possibility. 'Alphabet Logo' is a striking celebration of this language, showcasing over 500 logos built from the fundamental building blocks of communication: letters. In the hands of masterful designers, these familiar forms become vessels of meaning, distilled and reimagined to speak volumes, sometimes with a single stroke.

This collection is more than a source of inspiration; it's a testament to the enduring power of simplicity and the elegance of restraint. Featuring work from some of the world's most respected design studios, including Pentagram, Bruce Mau Design, Wolff Olins, Bond Creative, Hype Type Studio, Stockholm Design Lab and many others, 'Alphabet Logo' demonstrates how form and function can align in bold, unexpected and beautiful ways.

Whether a single letter becomes the cornerstone of a global brand or a clever typographic twist gives rise to a new identity, each mark in this book represents a unique solution to a universal challenge: how to say more with less.

For designers, students, brand strategists and visual thinkers alike, this compendium serves not only as a catalogue of exceptional logos but as a masterclass in craft, concept and clarity. It invites us to look closer, think deeper and appreciate the limitless potential that lies within the simplest shapes. These are more than logos, they are ideas made visible, each one capturing a brand's spirit through the power of a single glyph.

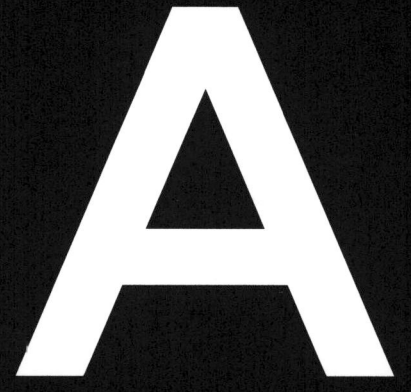

Anthology
Property development

Greenspace
thegreenspace.com
United Kingdom
2013

Anthropos
Family office

Studio Echt
studioecht.com
Slovakia
2017

Aroha Silhouettes
Jewellery design

We Are Branch
wearebranch.com
Canada
2011

**National Arts Council Singapore
& National Library of Singapore**
Cultural statutory board

studioKALEIDO
studiokaleido.net
Singapore
2014

A

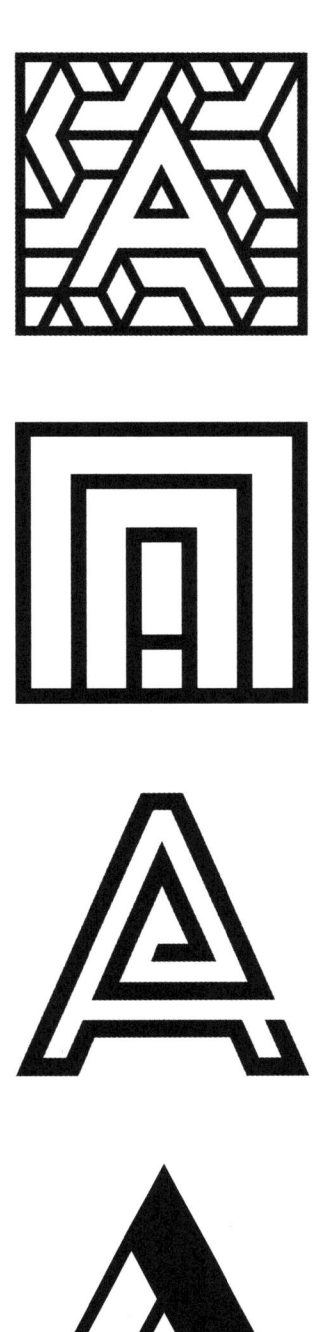

Architecture Centre Devon & Cornwall
Advocacy and support for architecture
& the built environment

Two
United Kingdom
twodesign.co.uk
2007

Arbenigol
Property development consultancy

Actual Studio
actual-studio.co.uk
United Kingdom
2013

Ashbys Sales & Lettings
Sales & lettings agents

Believe in®
believein.co.uk
United Kingdom
2010

Assembly
3D visualisation

SocioDesign
sociodesign.co.uk
United Kingdom
2013

A

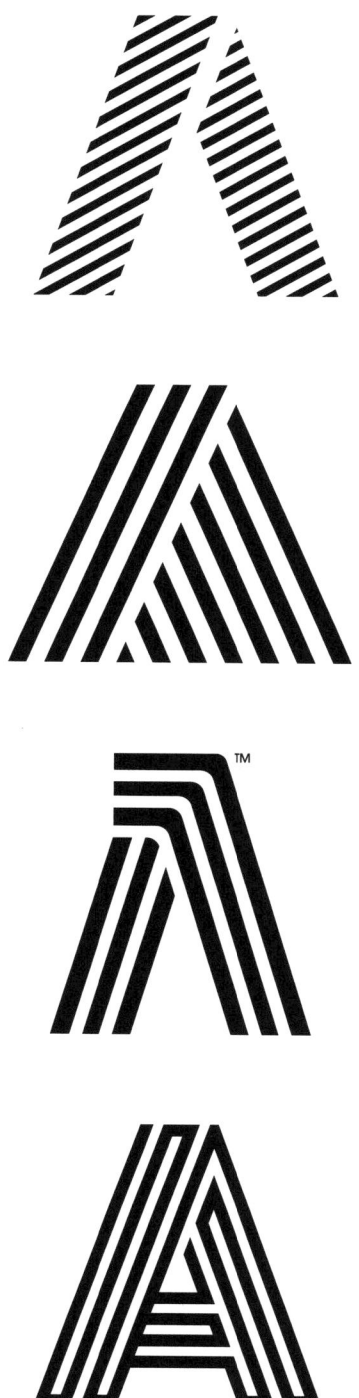

AirportTips
Online resource for airport information

Sali Tabacchi Inc.
salitabacchi.com
USA
2012

Awestruck Cider
Alcoholic drinks

Buddy
buddycreative.com
United Kingdom
2014

Disability Performance Austria
Platform to build up disability
confidence across company
& industry lines

Studio Es
studio-es.at
Austria
2014

Actionable
Technology training tools
for businesses

Underline Studio
underlinestudio.com
Canada
2016

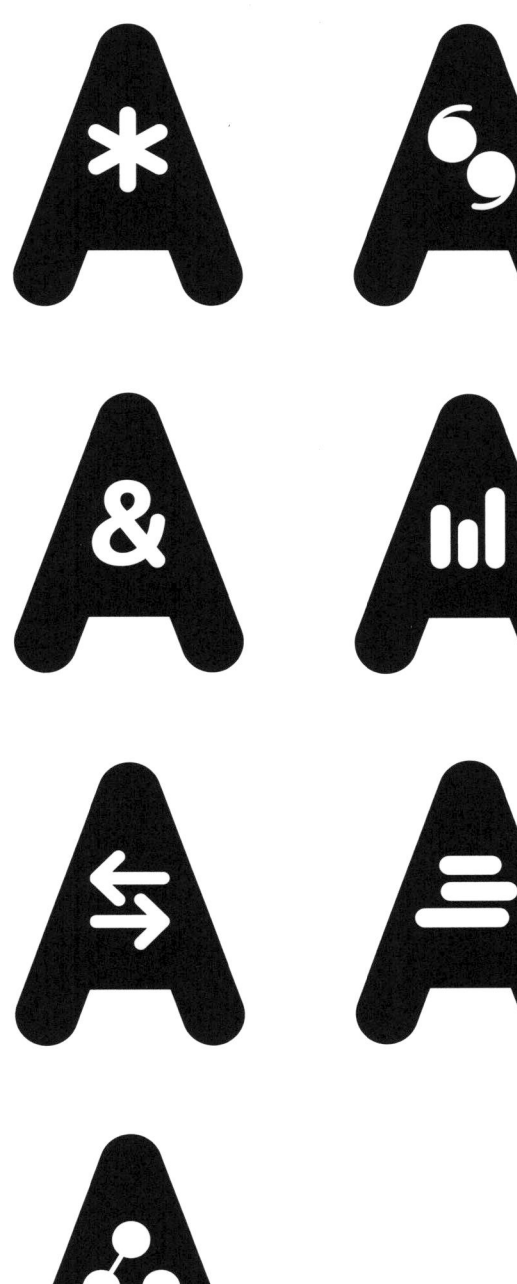

Airtime Productions
Film company

Nicklas Haslestad
nicklashaslestad.com
Norway
2013

Aleksa
Online gallery

SocioDesign
sociodesign.co.uk
United Kingdom
2014

Agenda
Online trip planner

Brandberry
brandberry.net
Russia
2012

Arralis
Space technology

AVB Brand
avb-brand.com
United Kingdom
2013

A

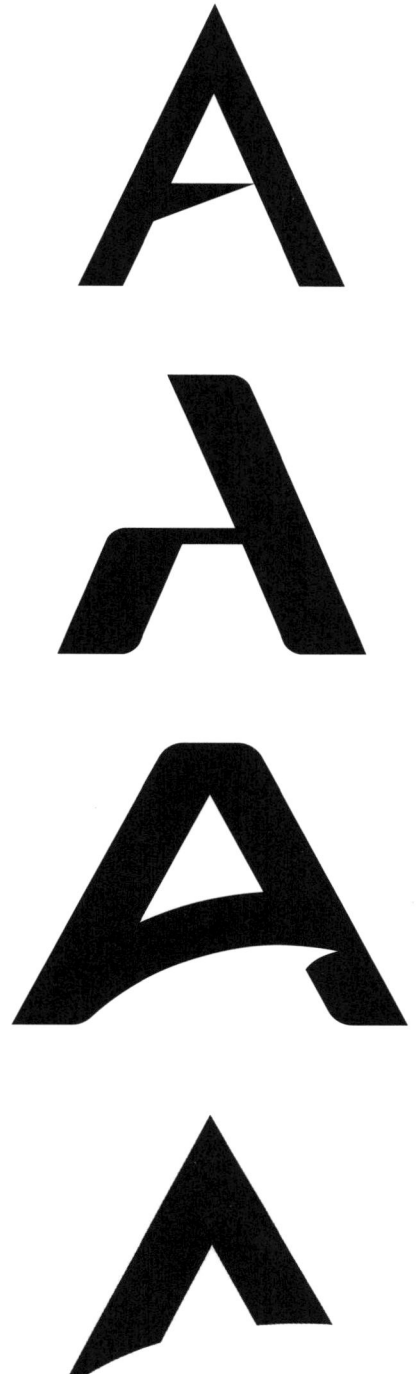

Archetype Architects
Architectural firm

BRNVD®
brvnd.com
Bulgaria
2021

Agulha
Textile solutions

Epiforma
epiforma.com
Portugal
2014

Après
DJ & producer

I See Sea
iseesea.co.uk
United Kingdom
2014

AAAPVP
Argentine Association of Street
& Outdoor Advertising Agencies

diseñollosa
diseñollosa.com.ar
Argentina
1995

A

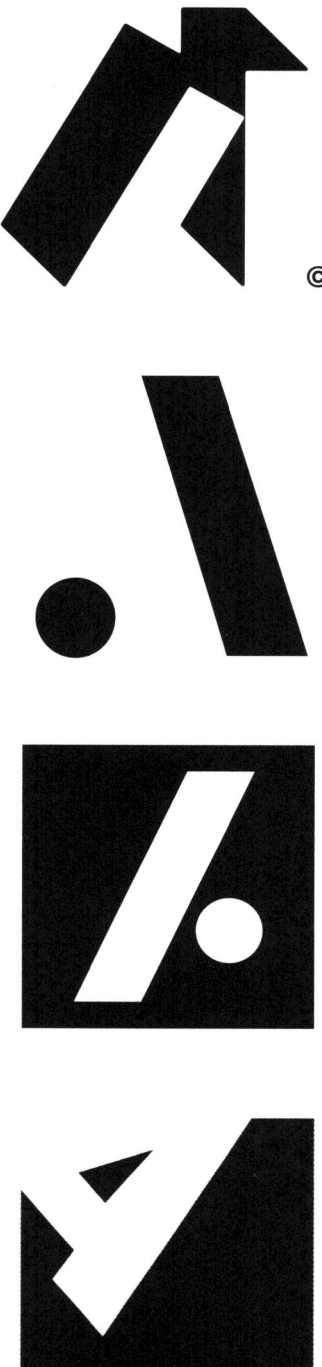

Actionable Analytics
Quantitative analysis

SocioDesign
sociodesign.co.uk
United Kingdom
2014

Attido　　　　　　　　　　　　　　　　　　　　A
Information & communications
technology

Bond Creative Agency
bond.fi
Finland
2011

Great Alpine Road
Tourism Victoria

Sadgrove Design
sadgrove.com
Australia
1998

Arcas
Architecture & urbanism

Chilli
chilli.be
Belgium
2013

Arbor for IQHQ
Science real estate

Mubien Brands & Workshop Built
mubien.com
USA
2022

Partido Andalucista
Political party

Cruz Novillo
cruznovillo.comstudio.com
Spain
1996

A

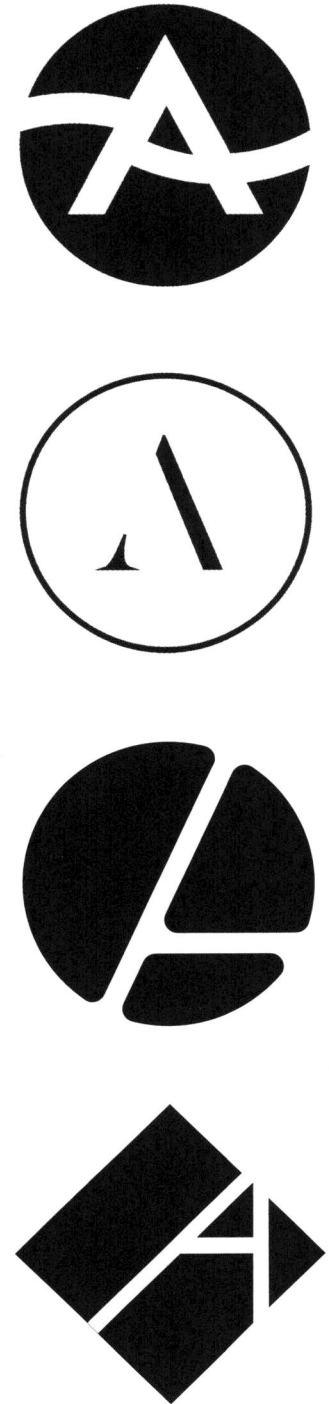

Add Studio
Graphic design

Add Studio
addstudio.se
Sweden
2013

AutoAvenue
Used car & motorcycle dealer

common graphic
common-graphic.com
Japan
2009

Askin'
Digital consultation with
dermatologists

Mission AS
mission.no
Norway
2019

Adaptfy
Data solutions

Metyis Design Studio
metyis.com
Netherlands
2020

A

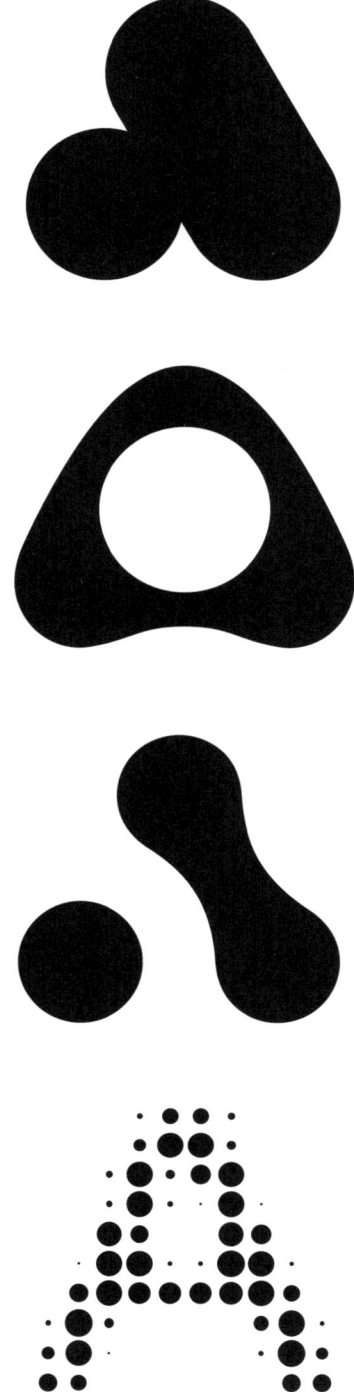

Ambient Group
Home technology

Studio Brave
studiobrave.com.au
Australia
2013

Adventure Films
Independent film production
company based in Luxembourg

Sam Lane
samlanedesign.co.uk
Luxembourg
2014

**PIKDAT (People I Know
Do Awesome Things)**
Culture website

Sam Flaherty Creative
samflahertycreative.com
New Zealand
2012

Fundacion Antonio Camuñas
Architecture foundation

Cruz Novillo
cruznovillo.com
Spain
1989

A

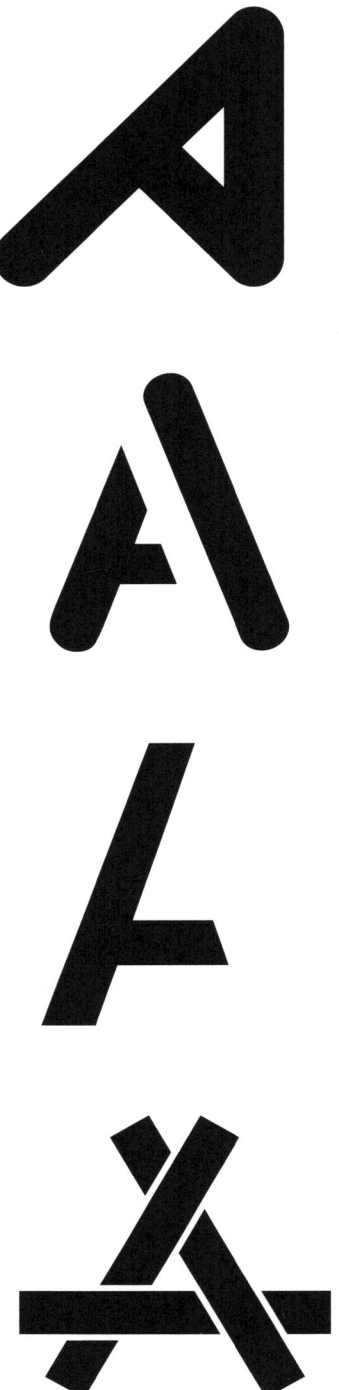

Arzabal
Gastronomy

Erretres Diseño y Comunicación
erretres.com
Spain
2013

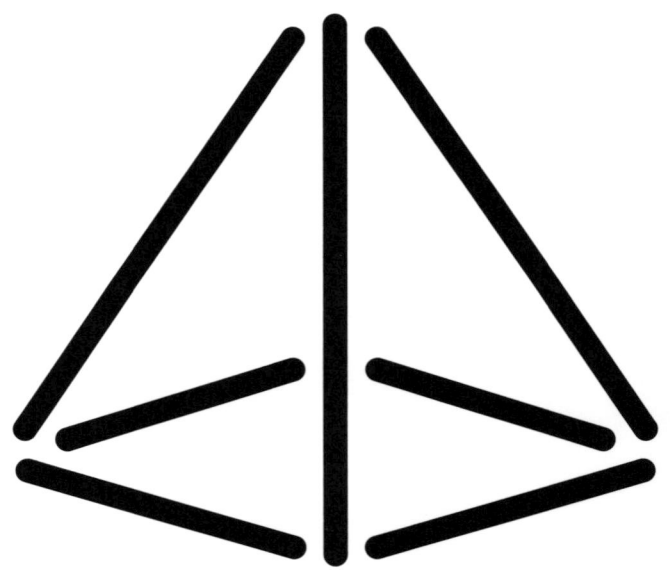

Fundación Antonio Machado
Antonio Machado foundation

A

Cruz Novillo
cruznovillo.com
Spain
1976

Åhlens
Department store

Stockholm Design Lab
stockholmdesignlab.se
Sweden
2012

AlphaHe
Tea range for men

Sam Flaherty Creative
samflahertycreative.com
United Kingdom
2013

Agaty for CRESCO REAL ESTATE a.s.
Real estate development project

Studio Echt
studioecht.com
Slovakia
2019

ANY BANK
Fintech company

UDL
u-d-l.com
China
2019

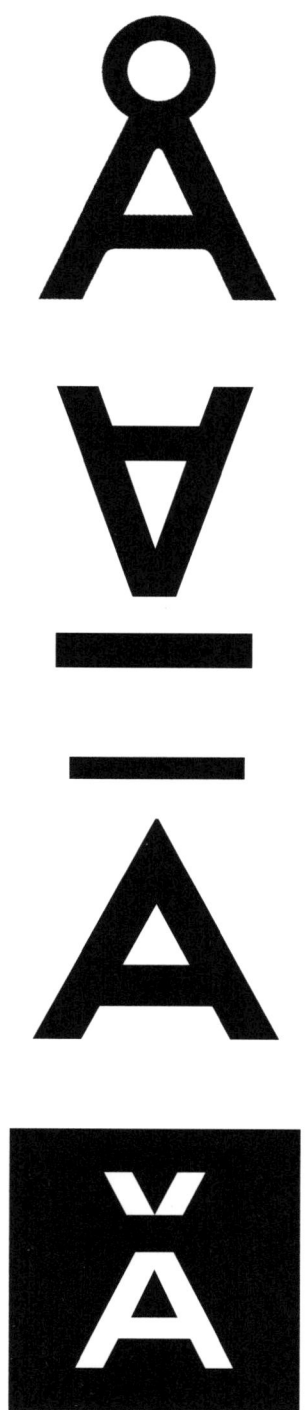

A

Ascent Technologies
Software developer

Brad Norr Design
bradnorrdesign.com
USA
2001

Archeology Alive
Educational organisation
providing practical archaeology
sessions for young people

Alphabetical
alphabeticalstudio.com
United Kingdom
2011

Apusana
Copywriting, SEO consulting
& affiliate marketing

Hahmo Design Oy
hahmo.fi
Finland
2011

Andersen
Event management

Brandberry
brandberry.net
Russia
2014

Archeology Alive
Educational organisation providing practical archaeology sessions for young people

Alphabetical
alphabeticalstudio.com
United Kingdom
2011

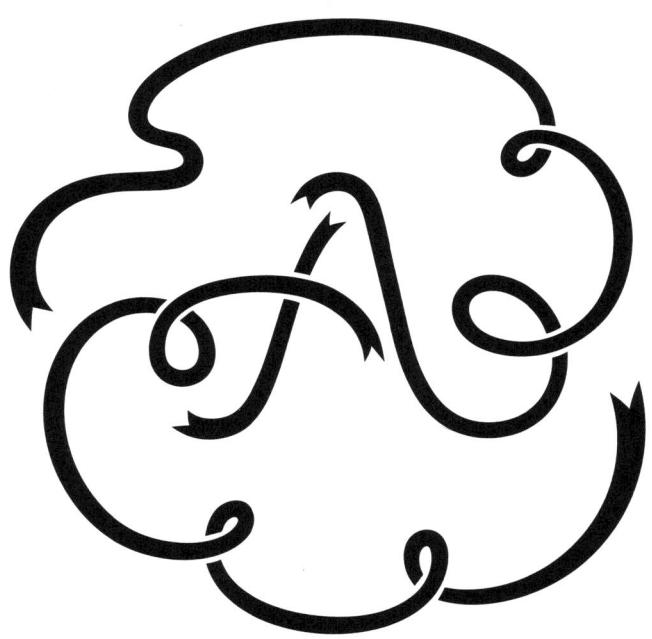

Astoria
Hotel

Stefan Kanchev
stefankanchev.com
Bulgaria
1950–1980

Aphrodite's
High-end food company

Midday
middaystudio.com
United Kingdom
2015

Ancoats Soap Co
Soap company

Angel & Anchor
angelandanchor.com
United Kingdom
2021

Arcology Apparel
Fashion

José Design
jose-design.nl
USA
2014

A

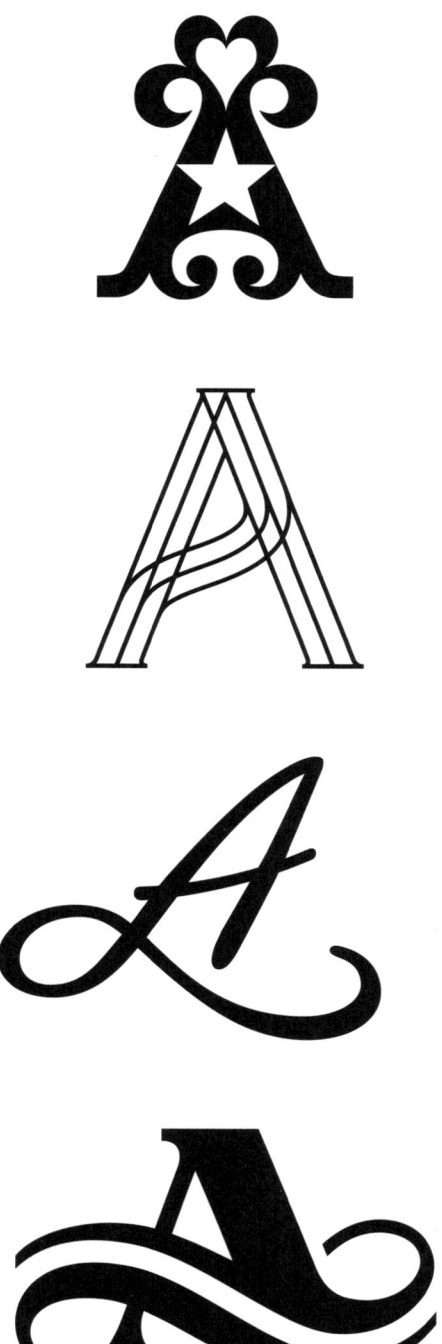

Andevine Wines
Winemaker

Co Partnership
co-partnership.com
Australia
2012

The Alverton A
Luxury hotel

Friends
designbyfriends.co.uk
United Kingdom
2012–2013

Alpha Snowboards
Snowboard manufacturer

Lazaris
wearelazaris.com
USA
2013

ARROYO
Lawyer

Massa
thisismassa.com
Spain
2022

Atome
Digital finance platform

&Larry
andlarry.com
Singapore
2020

Asmblx
Industrial design

Büro Ink
bueroink.com
Germany
2020

A

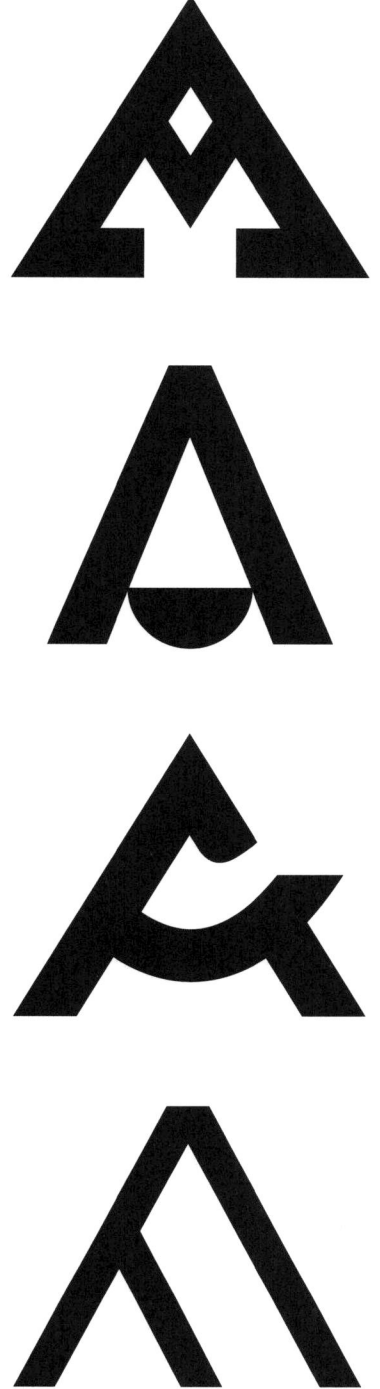

Artéria
Handmade leather products

Estudio Pum
estudiopum.com
Brazil
2012

Architecture
Magazine

Stefan Kanchev
stefankanchev.com
Bulgaria
1950–1980

European Space Agency – Ariane's Cup
Space technology

Eggers + Diaper
eggers-diaper.com
EU
2002

Arquinde
Architecture & engineering office

Cruz Novillo
cruznovillo.com
Spain
1969

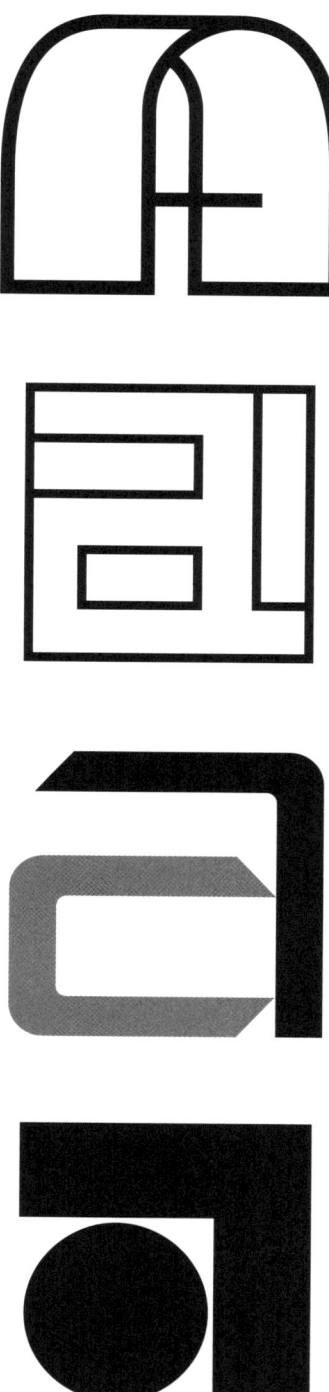

Allegion
Industrial security products & solutions

Lippincott
lippincott.com
USA
2013

Amp (Alphabet)
Live radio app

Koto
koto.studio
USA
2021

Audinate
Owner of Dante – audio & video over ethernet

Bedow
bedow.se
Sweden
2024

Autonomy
Digital art wallet

Berger & Föhr
bergerfohr.com
USA
2022

A

Allá Voy
Nearby shipping & other errands

El Paso, Galeria de Comunicación
elpasocomunicacion.com
Spain
2015

Ali Sharaf Photography
Photographer

Mash Creative
mashcreative.co.uk
Bahrain
2013

Amber Bear
Whole person mentorship
for courageous entrepreneurs

The Click
theclickdesign.com
United Kingdom
2023

A

Agricola
Restaurant

Mucca Design
mucca.com
USA
2013

A

Andaluz Audiovisual
Video production & colour correction

Plau
plau.co
Brazil
2013

Beats by Dr. Dre
Headphones & speakers

Pentagram / Brick Design
bricksf.com
USA
2006

Brand the Speaker
Branding for motivational speakers

Mode Design / Hans Bennewitz
modedesign.us
USA
2009

B

Bighorn Lodge
Ski lodge

Give Up Art
giveupart.com
Canada
2011

B Ferraz
Live marketing agency

Pedro Paulino
pedropaulino.com
Brazil
2014

Clinica Boixadera
Dentistry & oral medicine

Griselda Martí
griseldamarti.com
Spain
2012

The Bookery
Editorial

Albert Garrigó / Albert Romagosa
albertgarrigo.com
albertromagosa.com
Spain
2013

B

Bru Productions
Production company

Give Up Art
giveupart.com
South Africa / United Kingdom
2012

Aunt B's Blossoms
Florist & gardening boutique

The Hideout
thehideout.design
USA
2021

Beanstory
Subscription-based service
for direct to consumer beans

Blok Design
blokdesign.com
Canada
2022

B

53

Buildt
Quantity surveyors

Freytag Anderson
freytaganderson.com
United Kingdom
2014

Beight
Music / entertainment

Canefantasma
canefantasma.com
United Kingdom
2020

Atelier da Bouça
Architecture

R2
r2design.pt
Portugal
2008

Broadband Sports
Internet sports content provider

Gee + Chung Design
geechungdesign.com
USA
2001

B

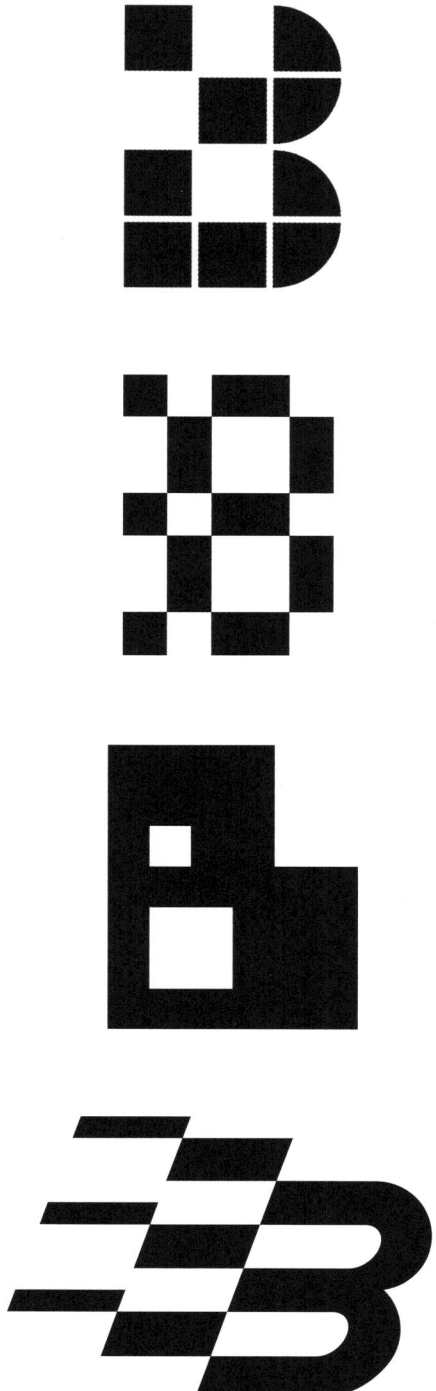

Bitmark
Blockchain technology

Berger & Föhr
bergerfohr.com
USA
2022

Balista Filmes
Film & motion design studio

Thiago Emmanuel / Studio Themm
themm.cc
Brazil
2022

Boreal Mountain Resort
Ski & snowboard resort

Hovercraft Studio
hovercraftstudio.com
USA
2013

Bosca
Furniture

Cruz Novillo
cruznovillo.com
Spain
1983

BOL
Clothing brand

indego design
indegodesign.com
Macao, China
2024

Bluebolt Networks
Materials resource

Alexander Isley Inc. Designers
alexanderisley.com
USA
2000

B

Bafra
Joinery & wood construction

Ibán Ramón + Dídac Ballester
ibanmasdidac.com
Spain
2006

Backstage
Casting platform for actors, models
& creators in the entertainment industry

High Tide
hightidenyc.com
USA
2019

BIFF
Independent film festival

Sam Lane
samlanedesign.co.uk
United Kingdom
2013

Brother Film Co.
Videography & production studio

I See Sea
iseesea.co.uk
United Kingdom
2014

B

Buckle for Dust
Theatre company

Radford Wallis
radfordwallis.com
United Kingdom
2008

Brandon Maxwell
Fashion designer

Alec Tear
alectear.com
United Kingdom
2018

Brighton Securities
Financial services

RNY
rny.is
USA
2014

Bookumenta
Digital storytelling

Barnéy Baker USA
barneybaker.co
Canada
2013

B

We Are Branch
Self-initiated

We Are Branch
wearebranch.com
USA
2013

Boabel
Screenplay writer

Maud
maud.com.au
Australia
2012

Biutiful
Hairdresser

Ole Büro
oleburo.com
Chile
2014

Being
Tech consultancy

Estudio Pum
estudiopum.com
Brazil
2017

B

Bundle
Curated maternity bags

The Company You Keep
tcyk.com.au
Australia
2013

Backstory
Documentary films

Nancy Wu Design
nancywudesign.com
USA
2011

Meulenhoff Boekerij
Publisher

Lava Design
lava.nl
Netherlands
2010

Little Black Book
Advertising

Freytag Anderson
freytaganderson.com
United Kingdom
2012

Bruschini Arquitetura
Architecture

Pedro Paulino
pedropaulino.com
Brazil
2013

Buena Onda Studio
Recording studio

Quim Marin
quimmarin.com
Spain
2011

Three Blokes
Pub & restaurant chain

The Click
theclickdesign.com
United Kingdom
2012

Bray & Slaughter
Construction

Mytton Williams
myttonwilliams.co.uk
United Kingdom
2014

B

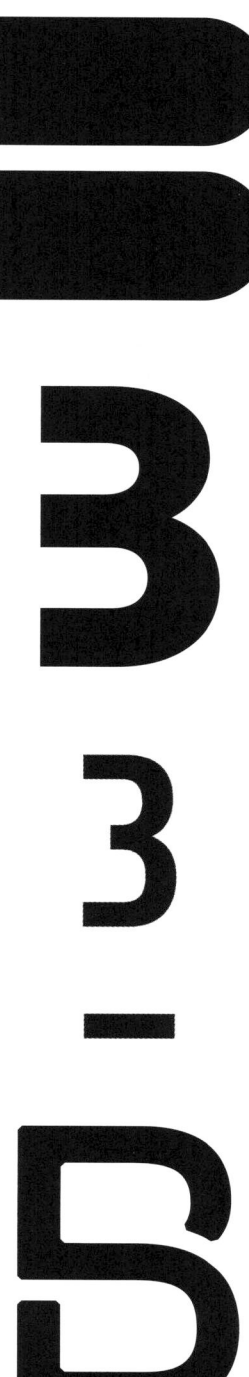

Brerra
Walk-in closets

Dmowski&Co.
dmowski.co
Poland
2018

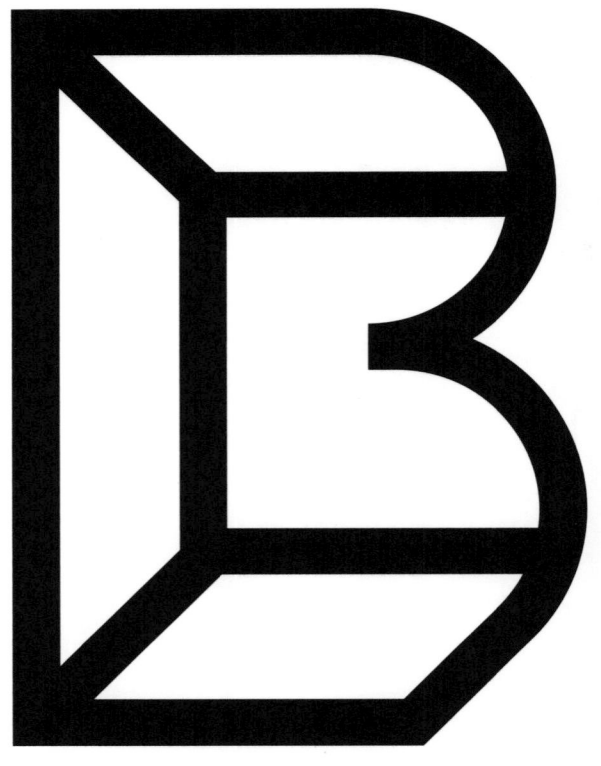

Bloc
Music festival

Give Up Art
giveupart.com
United Kingdom
2010

Brooksmart
Education

Fenton+Partners
fentonandpartners.com
United Kingdom
2021

Best
Foreign language courses

Pepe Cruz
cruznovillo.com
United Kingdom
1988

Blend
Cloud-based banking platform

Grammar
grammar.works
USA
2019

Beholder
Antique furniture

Give Up Art
giveupart.com
United Kingdom
2013

B

Schwarz zu Blau
Interior design

Bureau Hardy Seiler
hardyseiler.de
Germany
2020

Based on a True Story
Luxury travel

Rob Clarke Type Design & Lettering
robclarke.com
Australia
2006

Brash Brands
Brand consultancy

Rob Clarke Type Design & Lettering
robclarke.com
United Kingdom
2014

Bernards Market
High-end market

Strohl
strohlsf.com
USA
2004

Bumpkin
Restaurant

Irving & Co
irvingandco.com
United Kingdom
2012

Illustration
Karen Murray Design

Benefitfocus
Benefits management

Fuzzco
fuzzco.com
USA
2018

Petite Boutique
Lifestyle blog

New Royal Standard
newroyalstandard.com
United Kingdom
2008

Maison De Bruges
Artisan jam

Chilli
chilli.be
Belgium
2013

Butterfield Market
Groceries

Mucca Design
mucca.com
USA
2007

Belgravia London
London district

SomeOne
someoneinlondon.com
United Kingdom
2021

Juan Bengoa
Architecture & interior design studio

Aitor Baigorri
aitorbaigorri.com
Spain
2022

Brightlines
Translation services

Mytton Williams
myttonwilliams.co.uk
United Kingdom
2007

Bretherton Day
Executive recruitment

Radford Wallis
radfordwallis.com
United Kingdom
2009

B
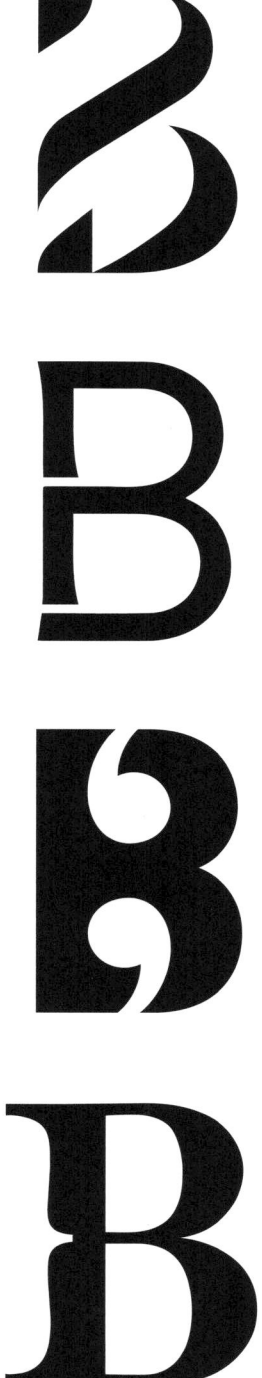

Bon Bot
Robotic ice cream bar

Add Studio
addstudio.se
Sweden
2020

Bog Eyed Books
Publisher

Baxter & Bailey
baxterandbailey.co.uk
United Kingdom
2016

Bravado
Music merchandise company
under Universal Music Group

High Tide
hightidenyc.com
USA
2017

Bancal
Agricultural credit bank

Cruz Novillo
cruznovillo.com
Spain
1971

B

Bowery
Farming

Koto
koto.studio
USA
2022

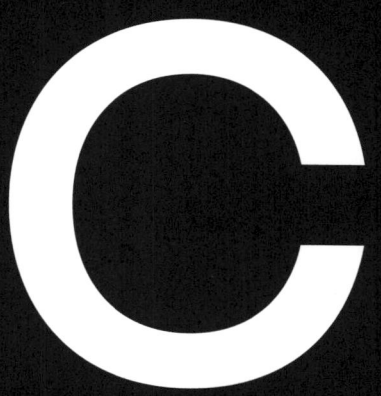

Commission for Rural Communities
Government agency

Mytton Williams
myttonwilliams.co.uk
United Kingdom
2006

Conrado Ceravolo Arquitetos
Architects

Pedro Paulino
pedropaulino.com
Brazil
2014

Capsule Skateboards
Skateboard manufacturer

Lazaris
wearelazaris.com
Greece
2017

Capélo
Hairdressers

Ateljé Altmann
ateljealtmann.com
Sweden
2010

C

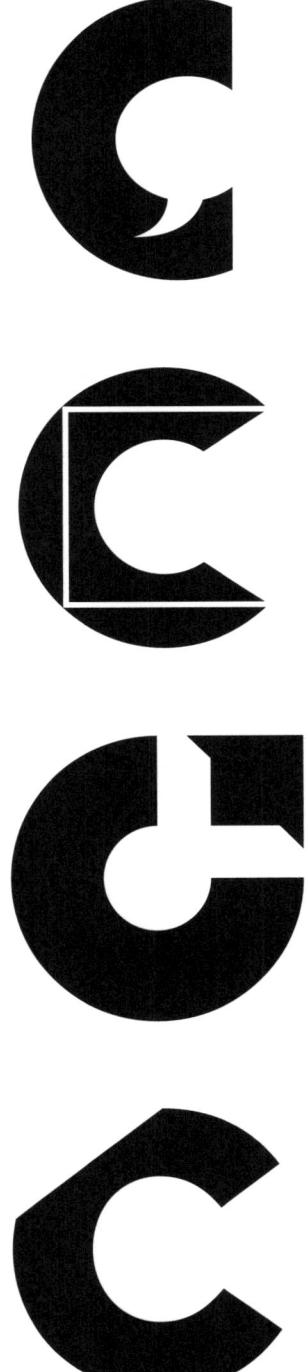

89

Australian Government, Department of Foreign Affairs
Government trade & diplomacy

Churchward/Melhuish
churchwardmelhuish.com
Australia
2013

Lisa Canning Interiors
Interior design

Sali Tabacchi Inc.
salitabacchi.com
Canada
2010

Superpedestrian, Inc
Electric bicycle

Math Practice / E Roon Kang
math-practice.org
eroonkang.com
USA
2013

C

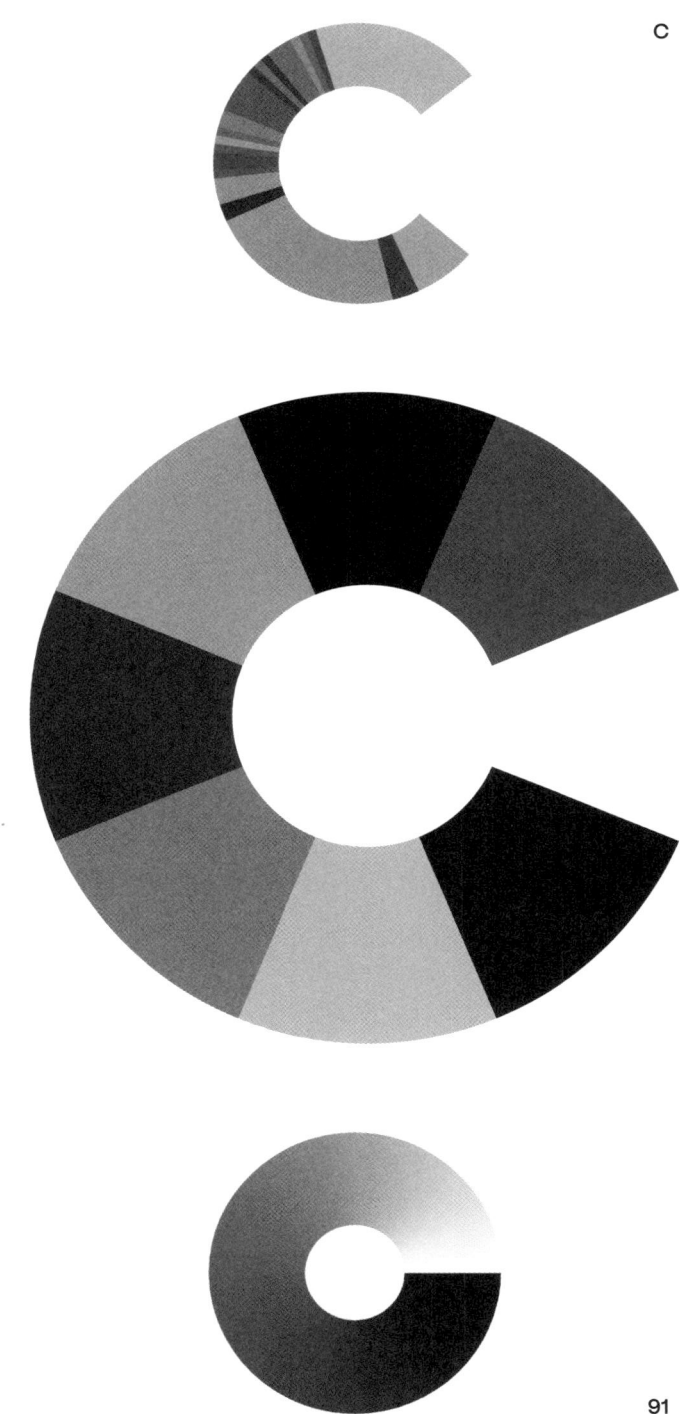

South West Festival Chorus
Choral group

Northbank
northbankdesign.co.uk
United Kingdom
2010

Creative Metrics
Client satisfaction consultation

Brad Norr Design
bradnorrdesign.com
USA
2000

Great British Chefs
Food & beverages

Hat-Trick Design
hat-trickdesign.co.uk
United Kingdom
2011

Curate International Collections
Fashion trade show

Bureau Hardy Seiler
hardyseiler.de
Germany
2019

C

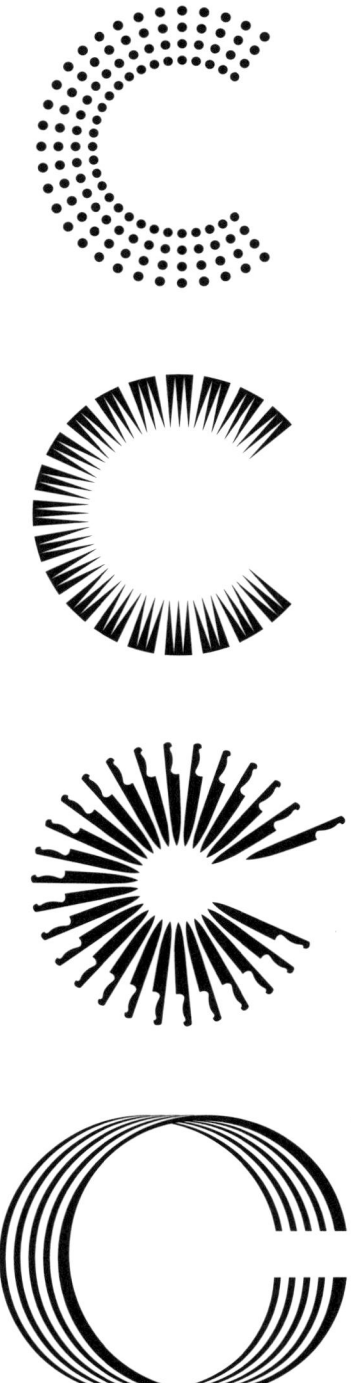

Casa Nostra
Wine bar

Kobe Design Center Inc.
hatto-graphico.com
Japan
2011

Carol Brodi
Jewellery designer

The O Group
ogroup.net
USA
2011

C

Cotonificio Lambrate
Cotton processing

Maurizio Milani
milanidesign.it
Italy
2001

Cope
Radio station

Cruz Novillo
cruznovillo.com
Spain
1993

College of Lake County
College

Essex Two
sx2.com
USA
2013

Catalyst Partners
Motivational speaker association

Essex Two
sx2.com
USA
2004

C

Chimimport
Chemical industry

Stefan Kanchev
stefankanchev.com
Bulgaria
1950–1980

El Terrat de Produccions, S.L.
Video production

Erretres Diseño y Comunicación
erretres.com
Spain
2012

**Ayuntamiento Segovia /
La Fábrica Gestión más Cultura**
Public organisation & culture

Erretres Diseño y Comunicación
erretres.com
Spain
2011

Compugraf
Computers

Cruz Novillo
cruznovillo.com
Spain
1977

C

Candy Cranks
Bike brand

Freytag Anderson
freytaganderson.com
Australia
2009

Ministère de la Culture et des Communications du Québec
Framework to integrate culture within the social, economic & environmental dimensions of sustainable development

Feed
studiofeed.ca
Canada
2011

Chorus Capital
Credit investment firm

Thomas Manss & Company
manss.com
United Kingdom
2011

Columbus Shopping Centre
Shopping centre

Hahmo Design Oy
hahmo.fi
Finland
1996

C

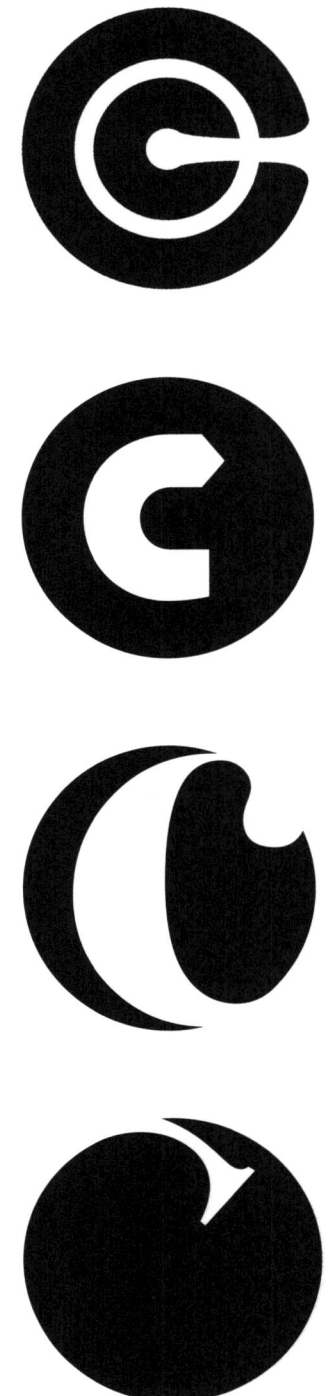

Create
Product design

Two Times Elliott
2xelliott.co.uk
United Kingdom
2013

Chénson
French restaurant

indego design
indegodesign.com
Macao, China
2024

Clarity
Financial advisor

Mash Creative
mashcreative.co.uk
United Kingdom
2013

Clarity
Financial advisor

Mash Creative
mashcreative.co.uk
United Kingdom
2013

C

Creative Services Group
Creative services

New Royal Standard
newroyalstandard.com
USA
2012

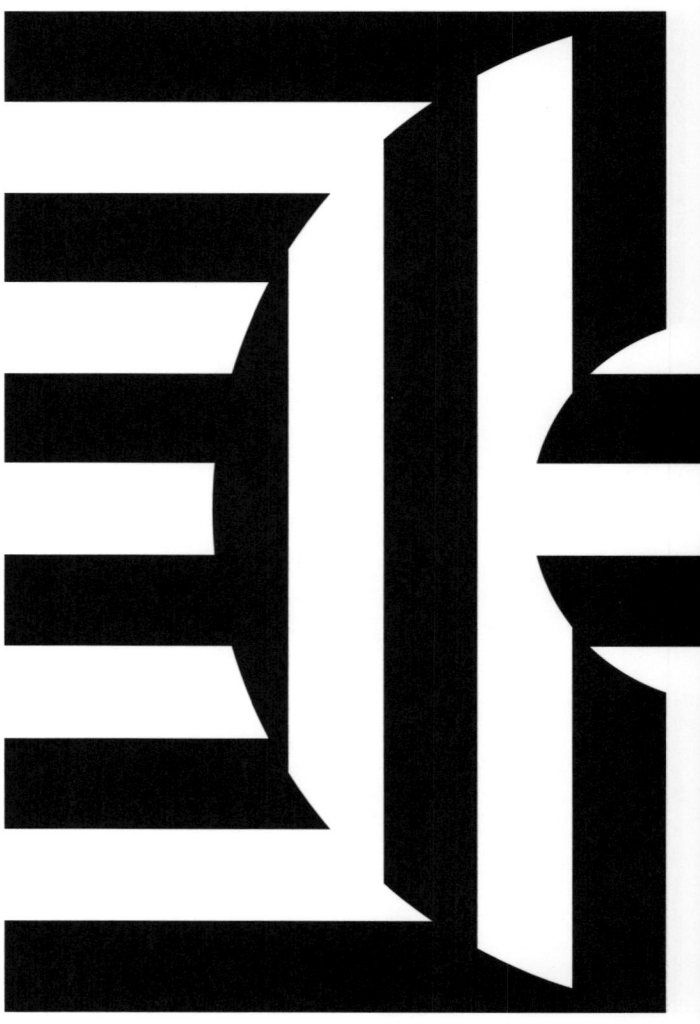

C

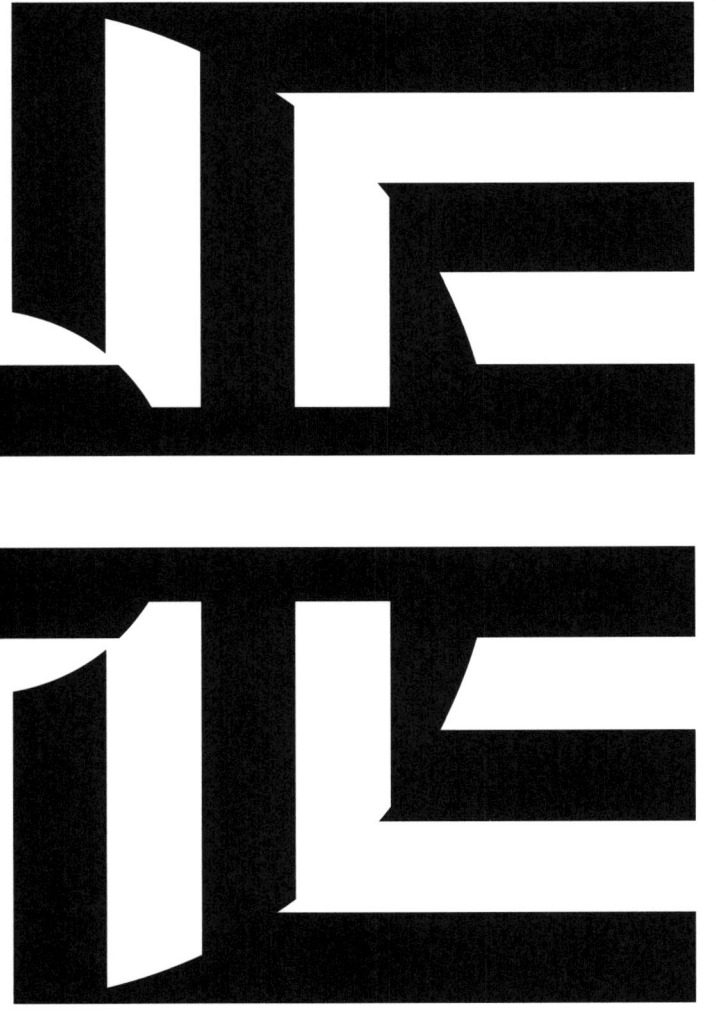

Continuity Ent
Event management

Mash Creative
mashcreative.co.uk
United Kingdom
2012

Circo Bar
Hospitality industry

Mytton Williams
myttonwilliams.co.uk
United Kingdom
2010

Coast Forecast
Surfing forecast application

Clarke Harris
clarkeharris.com
USA
2014

Cusp
Smart kitchen appliances

Mash Creative
mashcreative.co.uk
Australia
2014

C

NHS Camden & Camden Challenge
Health awareness

Mash Creative / Socio Design
mashcreative.co.uk
sociodesign.co.uk
United Kingdom
2012

Chehade Carter Diseño Interior
Interior design agency

Bienal Comunicación
bienal.mx
Mexico
2014

The Civic
Restaurant housed within
The Broadview Hotel

Blok Design
blokdesign.com
Canada
2018

Calitho
Printers

Brick Design
bricksf.com
USA
2012

C

ChoiceMap
Strategic consulting

Berger & Föhr
bergerfohr.com
USA
2014

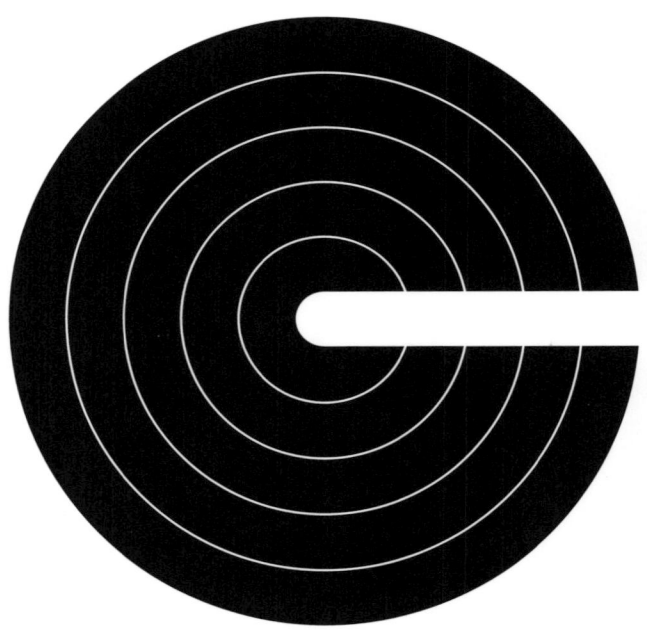

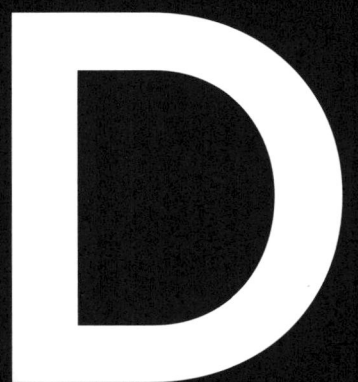

Denica – Haskovo
Fashion house

Stefan Kanchev
stefankanchev.com
Bulgaria
1950–1980

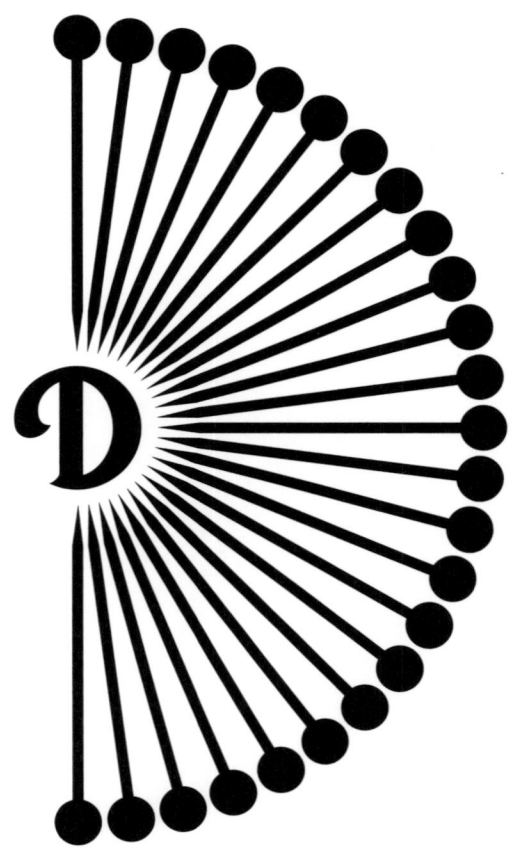

Bodegas Duratón
Winemaker family

D

Studio Fernando Gutierrez
fernandogutierrez.co.uk
Spain
2007

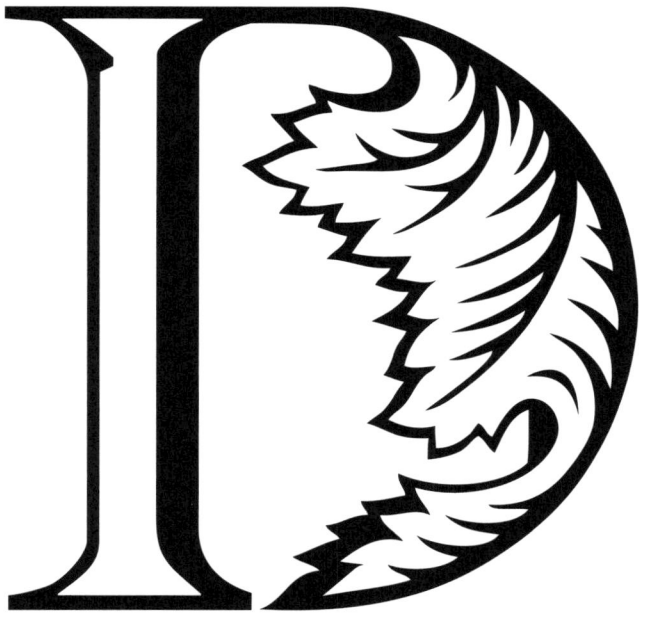

Demand Media
Content & social media

Manual
manualcreative.com
USA
2013

Devnya
Chemical industry

Stefan Kanchev
stefankanchev.com
Bulgaria
1950–1980

dottely
Marketing directory

AG Design Agency
agdesignagency.com
Greece
2021

D

Detour
Immersive, location-aware
audio walks

Strohl
strohlsf.com
USA
2014

D-sotto
Music club

Matteo Bartoli – Graphic Design Studio
matteobartoli.com
Italy
2013

Conversations in Design, sub-brand of the Interior Design Show
Lectures on the topic of design

Sali Tabacchi Inc.
salitabacchi.com
Canada
2010

Dalton Uehara
Multi-disciplinary creative

Pedro Paulino
pedropaulino.com
Brazil
2012

Dance Base
Scotland's national centre for dance

Touch
thetouchagency.co.uk
United Kingdom
2022

Decaria Builders
Custom home builder

Berger & Föhr
bergerfohr.com
USA
2022

D

119

West of England Design Forum
Networking group

Mytton Williams
myttonwilliams.co.uk
United Kingdom
2012

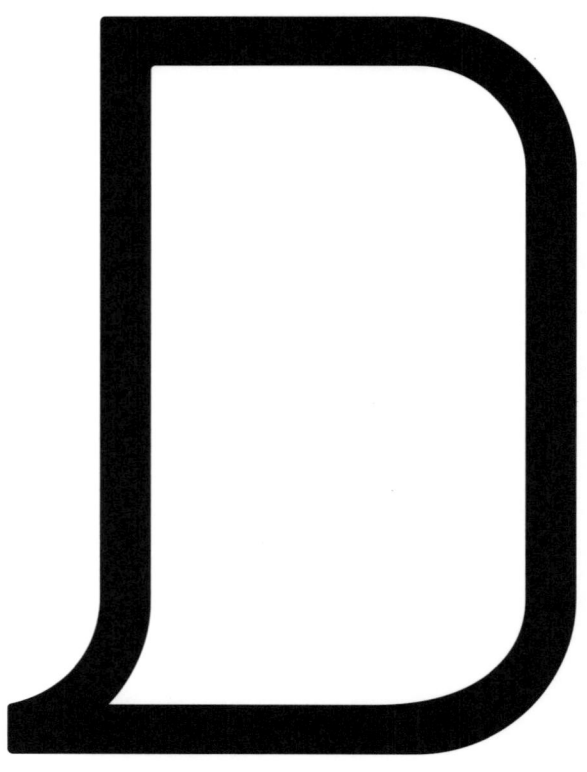

Distil Studio
Self-initiated

Distil Studio
distilstudio.co.uk
United Kingdom
2011

D

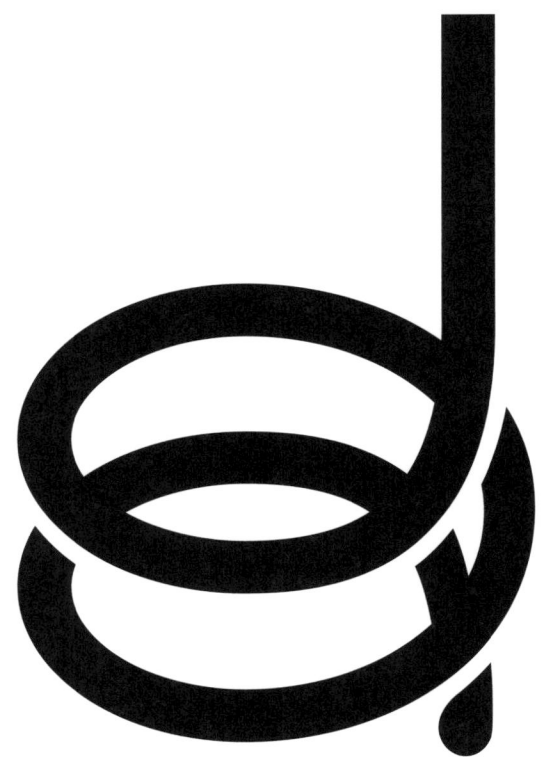

Diafragmas
Photography

Enrique Puerto
enrikepuerto.com
Mexico
2020

dCode
Stock music management

Edgar Bak Studio
edgarbak.info
Poland
2011

Doornroosje
Poppodia

studio another day
studioanotherday.nl
Netherlands
2014

EuropaType
Type design studio & online platform

Fabian Leuenberger
fabianleuenberger.com
Switzerland
2012

ECO-UTAN
Fundraiser for protecting
orangutans by fees collected
from disposing of expired fire
extinguishers

common graphic
common-graphic.com
Japan
2010

Energy
Software

Brandberry
brandberry.net
USA
2014

Emerge
Music license & promotion

Accept & Proceed
acceptandproceed.com
United Kingdom
2011

E

Electroimpex Sofia
Electrical goods

Stefan Kanchev
stefankanchev.com
Bulgaria
1950–1980

Essence Music
Record label

Duane Dalton
duanedalton.com
Brazil
2014

Envirowise
Environmental & drainage solutions

Grafiky
grafiky.co.uk
United Kingdom
2013

EOST2D / NHS Scotland
Type 2 diabetes programme

Touch
thetouchagency.co.uk
United Kingdom
2020

E

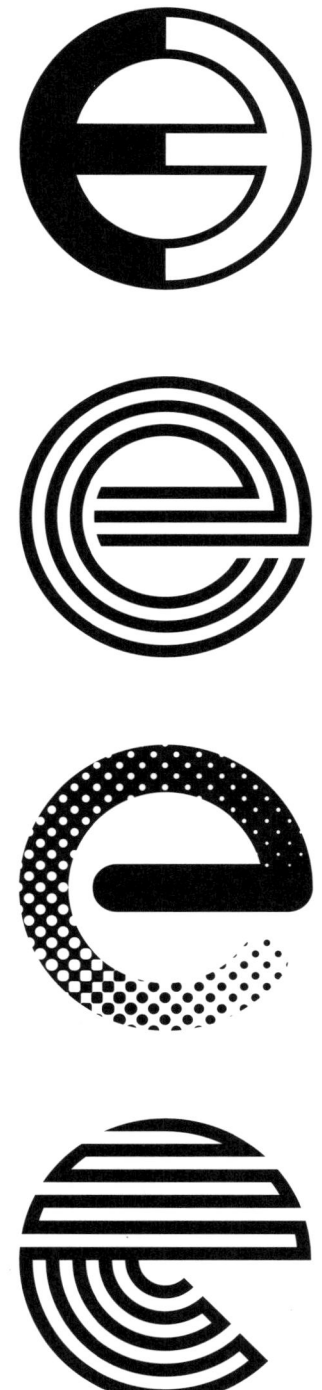

Euromar
Import & export

Milani Design
milanidesign.it
Italy
1980

Eleven
People management & training software

Telling Stories
tellingstories.co.uk
United Kingdom
2014

Plant Elektronika
Electronics

Stefan Kanchev
stefankanchev.com
Bulgaria
1950–1980

Easton and Otley College
A land-based studies college

The Click
theclickdesign.com
United Kingdom
2017

E

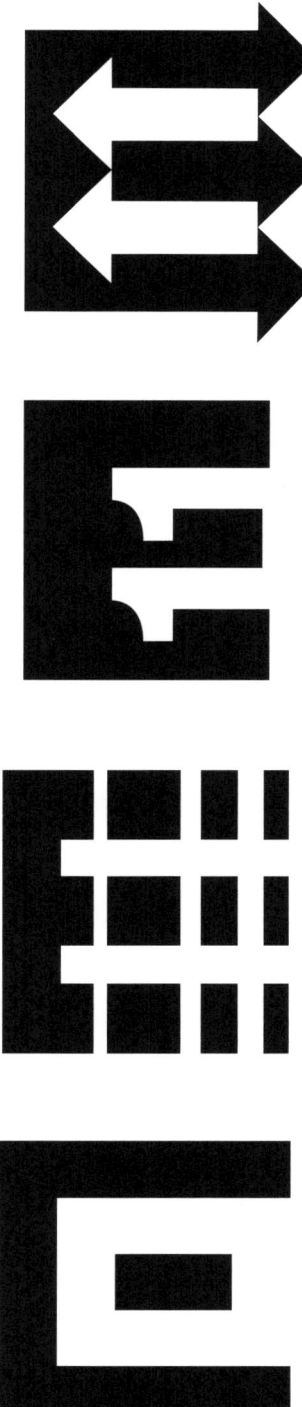

131

Visual Enterprise
Information architecture

Mash Creative
mashcreative.co.uk
Germany
2013

Have No Equal
Clothing label

E

JB Studio
jordanblyth.com
United Kingdom
2008

Head East
A flagship brand for the East of England

The Click
theclickdesign.com
United Kingdom
2021

Cinex
Film production

Ateljé Altmann
ateljealtmann.com
Switzerland & Netherlands
2008

Ergomaster
Adjustable desk frames

Dmowski&Co.
dmowski.co
Poland
2021

E2Designlabs
Water sensitive urban design

inkahoots
inkahoots.com.au
Australia
2011

E

Ehrnst consulting
Retail consulting

Edgar Bak Studio
edgarbak.info
USA
2020

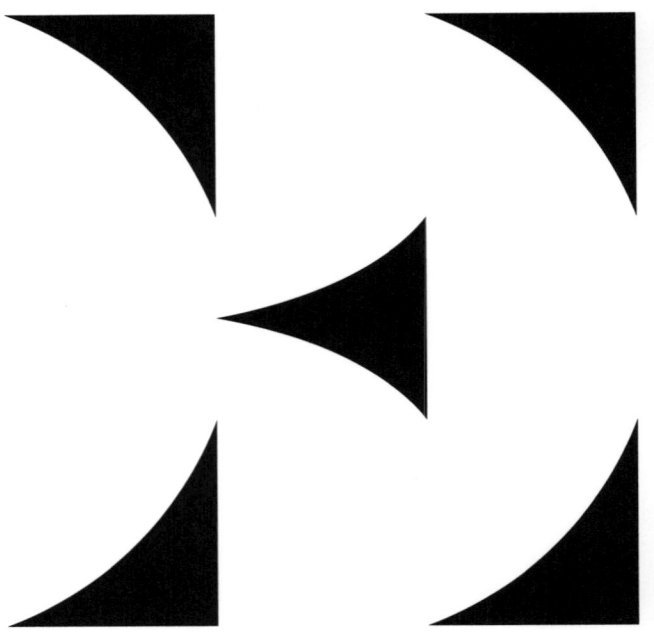

Esicma
Audiovisual production company

Cruz Novillo
cruznovillo.com
Spain
1989

Echobox
Intelligent publishing service
that increases traffic for news
publishers

1910 Design & Communication
weare1910.com
United Kingdom
2014

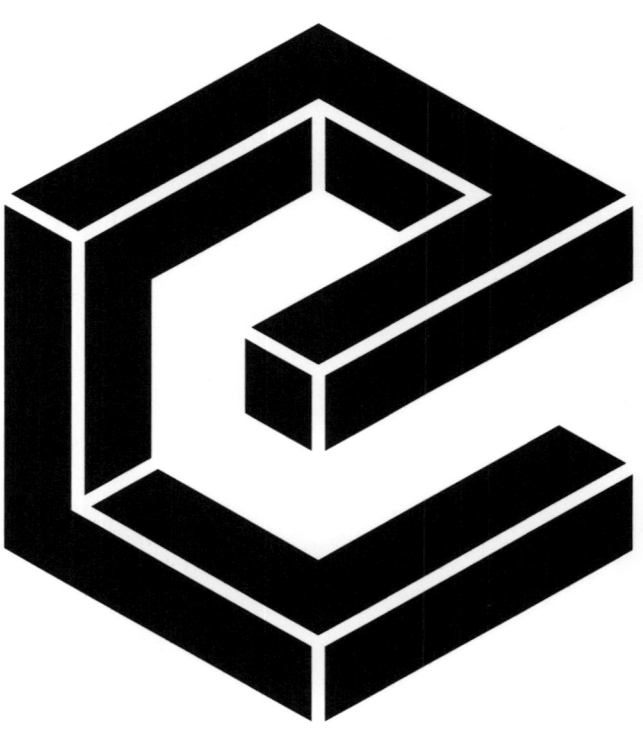

Fresco
Co-working office

Matteo Bartoli – Graphic Design Studio
matteobartoli.com
Italy
2011

Fazer
Project management app

Metyis Design Studio
metyis.com
Spain
2022

Flish
Satellite communications

AVB Brand
avb-brand.com
United Kingdom
2013

Freshaspect
IT service

Tomasz Biskup
tomaszbiskup.com
Poland
2014

F

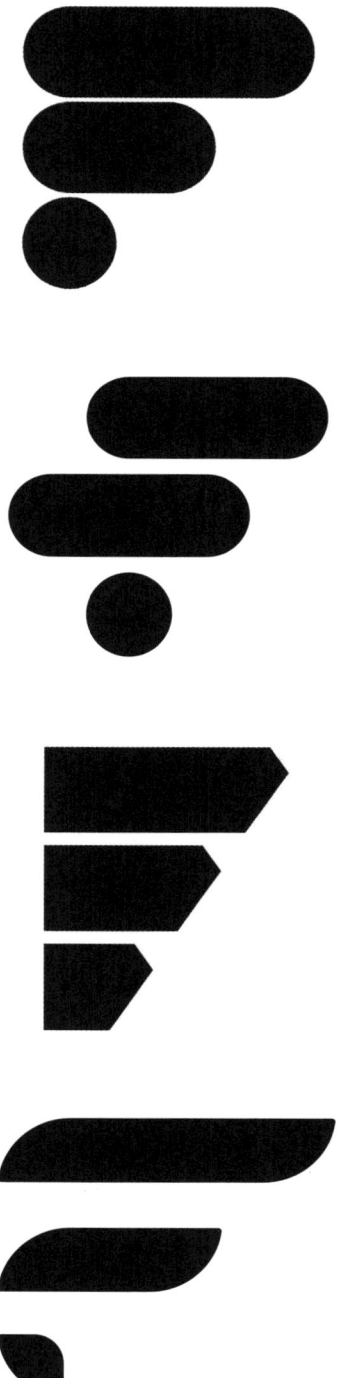

Sans Form
T-shirt company

Duane Dalton
duanedalton.com
Italy & USA
2014

Flaner
Mobile application

Brandberry
brandberry.net
Russia
2014

Fusions
Australian network of clay
& glass artists

inkahoots
inkahoots.com.au
Australia
2005

Ida Faldbakken
Freelance project manager

Nicklas Haslestad
nicklashaslestad.com
Norway
2013

F

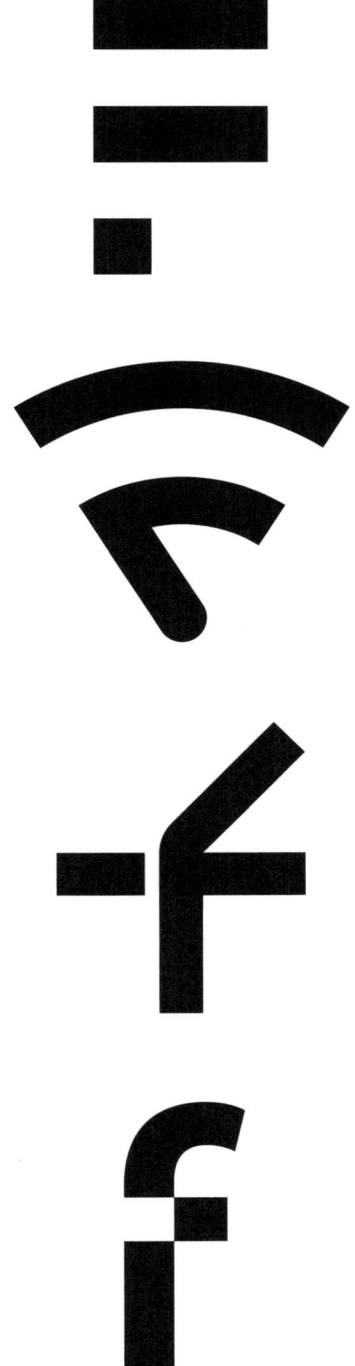

143

Future Materials
Consultancy

Design by Toko
designbytoko.com
The Netherlands / Australia
2022

FabricNano
Biotechnology company

Ascend Studio
ascendstudio.co.uk
United Kingdom
2021

Frank
Window frames

Dmowski&Co.
dmowski.co
Norway
2015

Filma Porto
Porto film promotor

This is Pacifica
thisispacifica.com
Portugal
2021

F

145

Fruitmarket
Contemporary art space

Touch
thetouchagency.co.uk
United Kingdom
2021

Fortified Branding
Marketing

Abby Haddican Studio
abbyhaddican.com
USA
2023

FeralFile
Generative art gallery

Berger & Föhr
bergerfohr.com
USA
2022

FREIRAUM
Space for seminars, meetings, conferences, workshops or workrooms

Jens Windolf
jenswindolf.de
Germany
2015

F

Future and Found
Interior designers & retailer

Horse
horse-studio.com
United Kingdom
2013

Freitags
Weekly music event

Teacake Design
teacakedesign.com
Germany
2010

F

Fascar
Shoe store

Pedro Paulino
pedropaulino.com
Brazil
2013

Fiorella
Floral design

Chris Pecora Makes Stuff
chrispecora.com
Canada
2014

Factual Fashion
Fashion blog

Jonathan Patterson
jonathanpatterson.com
2013
N/A

Foxtons
Estate agents

Rob Clarke Type Design & Lettering / Bear
robclarke.com
United Kingdom
2002

F

Fademesa
Art foundation

Cruz Novillo
cruznovillo.com
Spain
1986

The Folio Prize
Literature prize

Planning Unit
planningunit.co.uk
United Kingdom
2013

Frank Usher
Men's fashion

Mash Creative
mashcreative.co.uk
United Kingdom
2009

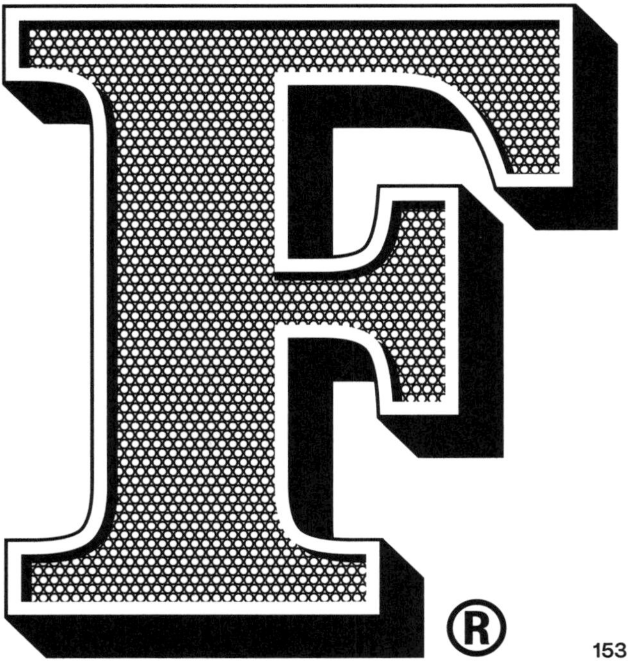

F

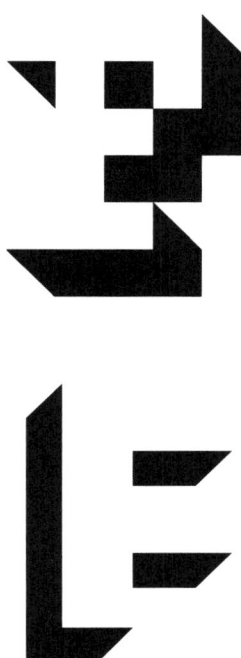

Friends of the Simon Stevin Institute for Geometry
Dutch institution focused on geometry

Boy Bastiaens
stormhand.com
The Netherlands
2008

Future Factory
Lead generation, new business & training

DutchScot
dutch.scot
United Kingdom
2022

FiberMark
Industrial materials

Lippincott
lippincott.com
USA
1997

Fraher
Architects

Freytag Anderson
freytaganderson.com
United Kingdom
2014

F

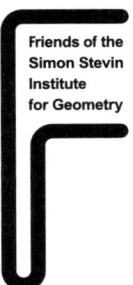

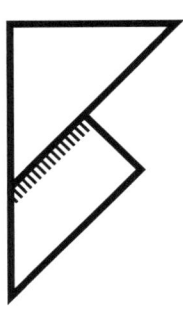

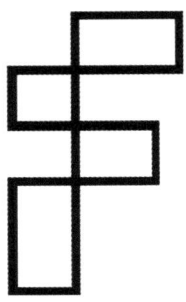

Los Angeles Times Food
Publishing

Abby Haddican Studio
abbyhaddican.com
USA
2023

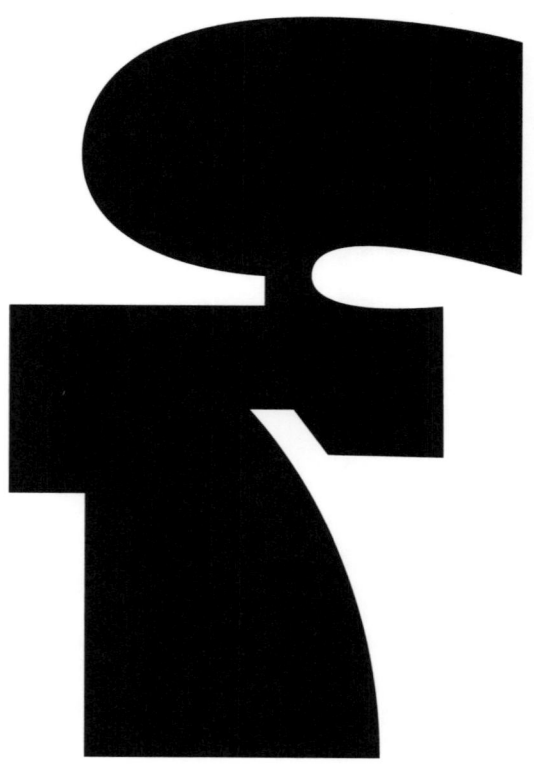

Filmosaurus Rex
Film production

Manasteriotti DS
manasteriotti.com
Croatia
2012

F

UOAK corp.
Fashion brand

Tetusin Design Office
tetusin.com
Japan
2010

Fable
Innovative pet product company

High Tide
hightidenyc.com
USA
2018

Fanthropology
Entertainment consultancy

Corey Holms
coreyholms.com
USA
2013

Fobe
Unlimited access to the latest it-bags

Bureau Hardy Seiler
hardyseiler.de
Germany
2021

F

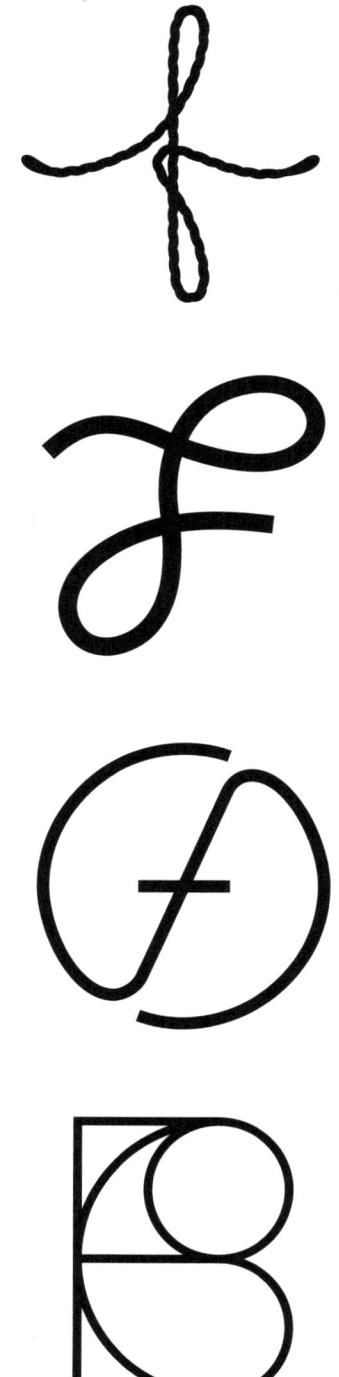

Future Nordic Design
Publishing

Ateljé Altmann
ateljealtmann.com
Sweden
2010

Gil Turner Arquitectos
Architectural firm

Lucas Gil Turner Branding & Design
lucasgilturner.com
Spain
2013

Garibaldi G
Lounge & wine bar

Designcriteria
designcriteria.it
Italy
2010

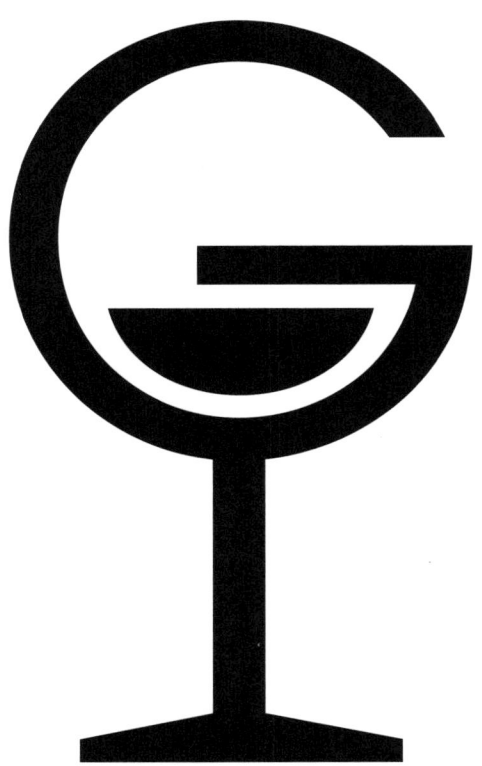

Gap
Clothing retailer

Manual
manualcreative.com
USA
2010

Glinomi
Aluminium accessories

Tomasz Biskup
tomaszbiskup.com
Poland
2014

Shipping Guru
Shipping & sea logistics

Werklig
werklig.com
Finland
2011

The Gallimaufry
Bar & restaurant

Ged Palmer
gedpalmer.com
United Kingdom
2012

G

Gaya Shoe Boutique
Shoe retail

Richard Baird
richardbaird.co.uk
Israel
2014

Garbett design
Self-initiated

Garbett Design
garbett.com.au
Australia
2013

Gaydio FM
Gay radio station

Studio DBD
studiodbd.com
United Kingdom
2012

Giraffage
Producer

Barnéy Baker USA
barneybaker.co
USA
2014

G

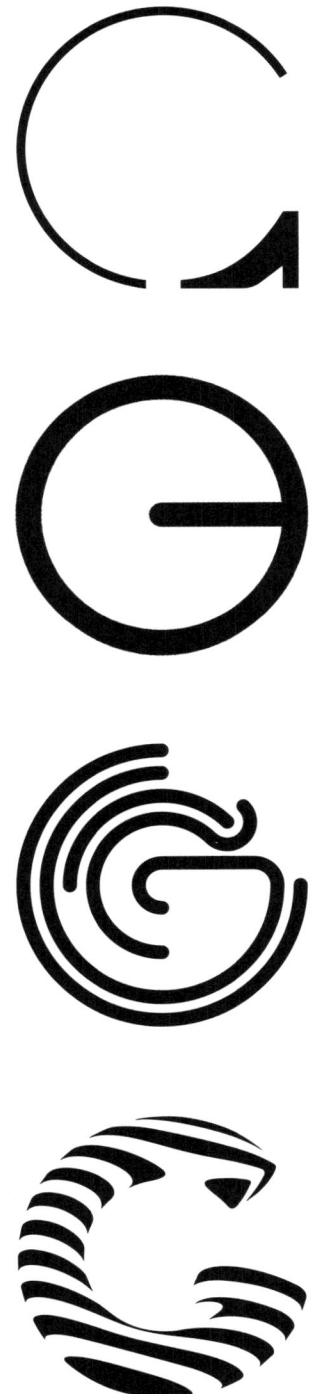

Lucas Gil Turner Branding & Design
Self-initiated

Lucas Gil Turner Branding & Design
lucasgilturner.com
Spain
2012

Galante
Builder and real estate
for apartments & offices

diseñollosa
diseñollosa.com.ar
Argentina
1985

Guld Arkitekter
Architects

Ateljé Altmann
ateljealtmann.com
Sweden
2012

Giropais
National money transfers

Cruz mas Cruz
cruznovillo.com
Spain
2011

G

Pascale Girardin
High-end dishware & architectural
design pieces for the luxury
hospitality industry

Feed
studiofeed.ca
Canada
2010

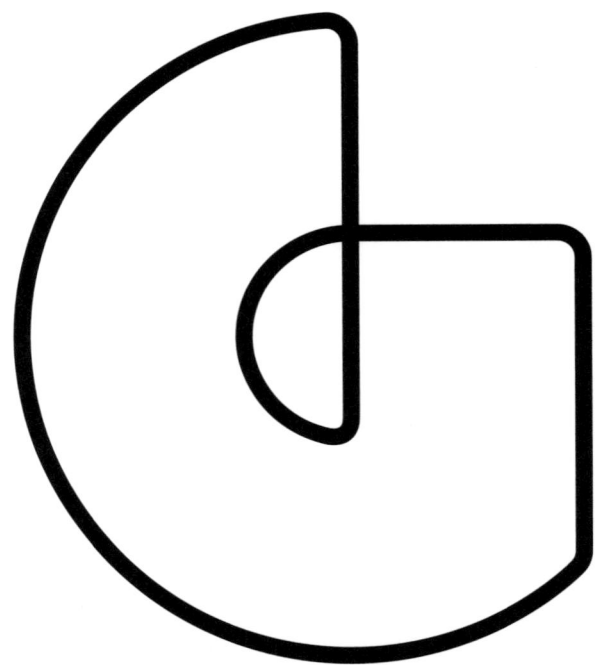

GetDressed
Women's retail

dng studio
dngstudio.com
Canada
2009

G

Gromia
Real estate

Emanuele Abrate
emanueleabrate.com
Italy
2021

Gressingham Foods
Speciality poultry

Rob Clarke Type Design & Lettering /
Elmwood
robclarke.com

United Kingdom
2012

Gott's Van & Car Service Centre
Car service centre

JB Studio
jordanblyth.com
United Kingdom
2011

Café Gelato
Italian Gelato

JB Studio
jb-studio.co.uk
United Kingdom
2015

G

La Galga
Restaurant & bar

Aitor Baigorri
aitorbaigorri.com
Spain
2023

The Gunmaker's Trust
Funds apprentices for young
gunstock carvers

Atelier Works
atelierworks.co.uk
United Kingdom
2001

Maxwell's Group for Guanabara
Bar & nightclub

Mash Creative
mashcreative.co.uk
United Kingdom
2012

Glossier
Cosmetic brand

Leslie David Studio
leslie-david.com
France
2014

G

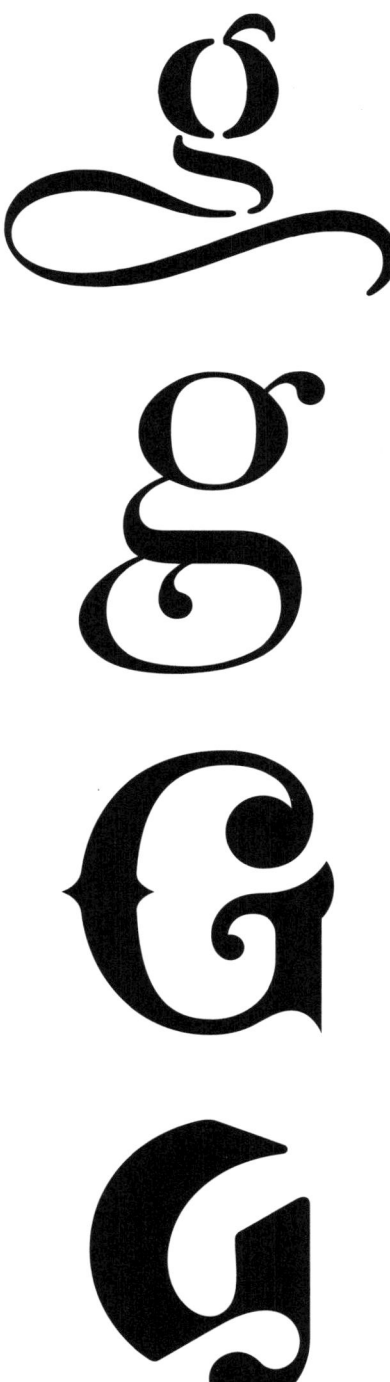

Goodcall
Global market research
& telemarketing

Christopher Doyle & Co.
christopherdoyle.co
Australia
2013

Grapes Consulting
Winemaker

Parallax Design
parallaxdesign.com.au
Australia
2005

Good Egg Books
Young adult publisher

Brad Norr Design
bradnorrdesign.com
USA
2005

G

GLOKIO
Complete system of vitamins &
minerals adjusted to women's needs

VORM lab
vormlab.com
Poland
2014

H

Hauptstadt
Online newspaper

Büro Destruct
burodestruct.net
Switzerland
2021

Hoyle
Card games

Studio Camo
studiocamo.com
USA
2011

Harmony
Bistronomy

Chilli
chilli.be
Belgium
2013

Hudson Shoe Agencies
Footwear

IYA Studio
iyastudio.co.uk
United Kingdom
2013

H

Hristo Nikov
Confectionery

Stefan Kanchev
stefankanchev.com
Bulgaria
1950–1980

HauteNature
Couture blog focused
on eco-friendly products

Celeste Prevost
designisfine.com
USA
2010

H

Hawksworth
Fine dining restaurant

Nancy Wu Design / Lightroom
nancywudesign.com
lightroomfx.com
Canada
2008

Hands
Live marketing agency

Pedro Paulino
pedropaulino.com
Brazil
2013

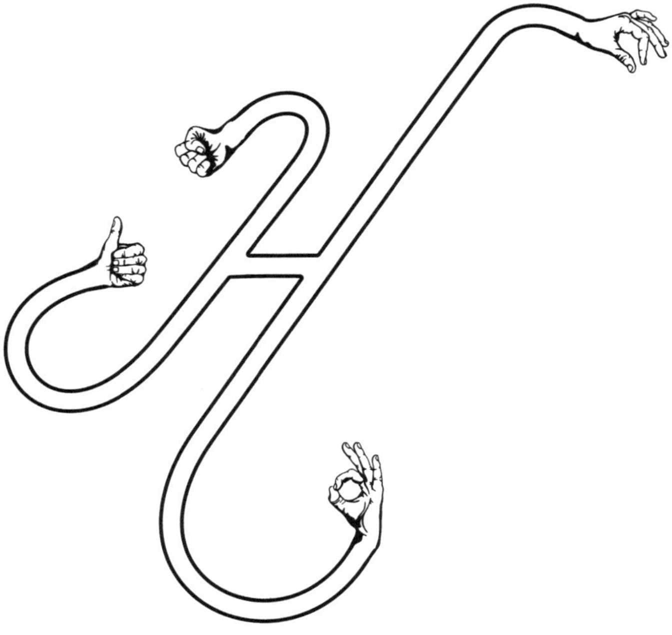

H

Horse
Self-initiated

Horse
horse-studio.com
United Kingdom
2012

Habiens
Neuroscience institute

BRBAUEN
brbauen.com
Brazil
2018

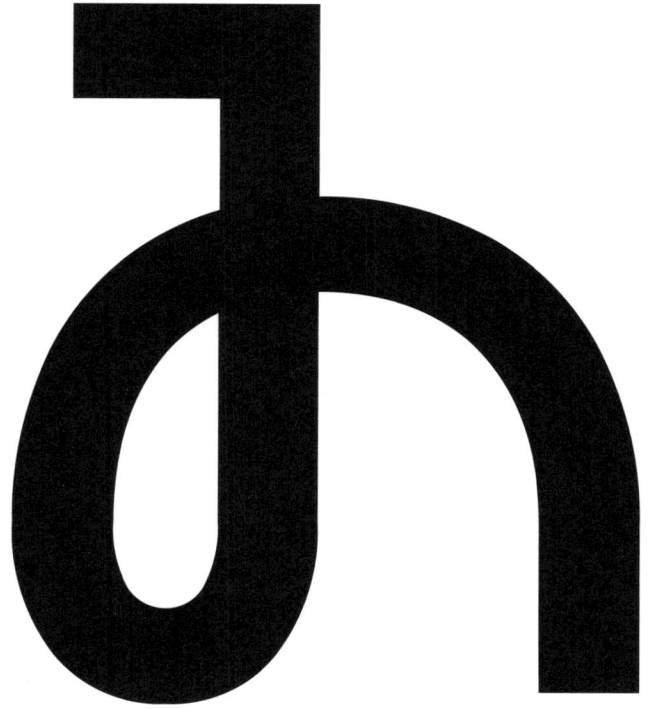

Swedish History Museum
Museum

Bold
boldstockholm.se
Sweden
2013

Hotopics
Social news blog

Lyam Bewry
lyambewry.co.uk
United Kingdom
2013

Hayashi Co. Ltd.
Electric & machinist hand tools

common graphic
common-graphic.com
Japan
2011

Home Storytellers
Organisation using the power of visual storytelling to amplify solutions to the refugee crisis

Carlos Galán Rubio
galanrubio.com
Spain
2018

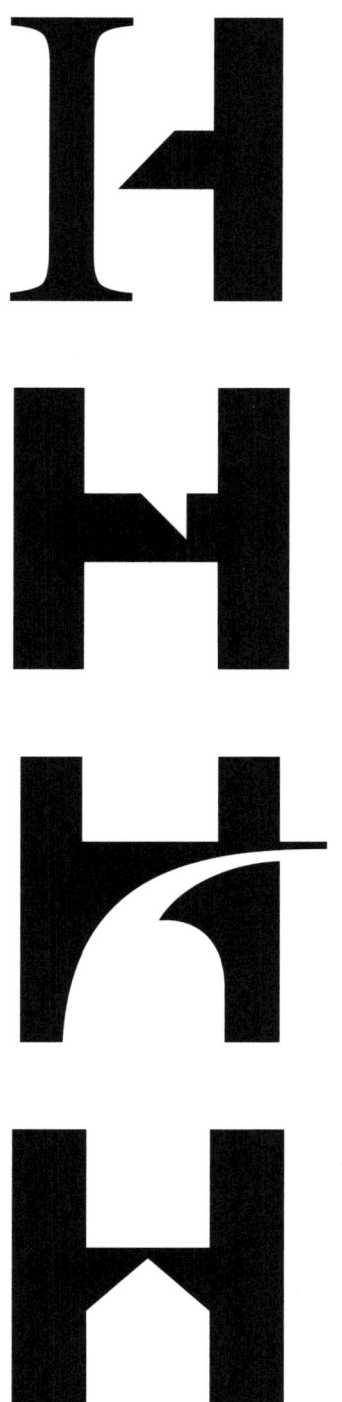

H

Hiking English
English school & translation studio

üla
ula.com.ar
Argentina
2016

Hutch
Gallery

Mash Creative
mashcreative.co.uk
United Kingdom
2008

Haringey Carers
Carers support service

JB Studio
jordanblyth.com
United Kingdom
2010

H

**The Foundation for Social
and Economic Initiatives (FISE)**
Organisation acting to increase
employment, especially among
professionally inactive groups

Edgar Bak Studio
edgarbak.info
Poland
2016

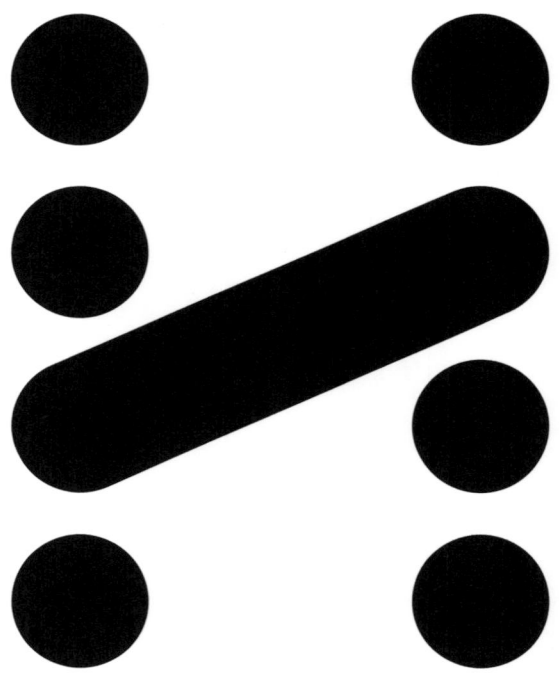

Haemopressin
Pharmaceutical

H

From Parts Unknown
frompartsunknown.co.uk
United Kingdom / Europe
2009

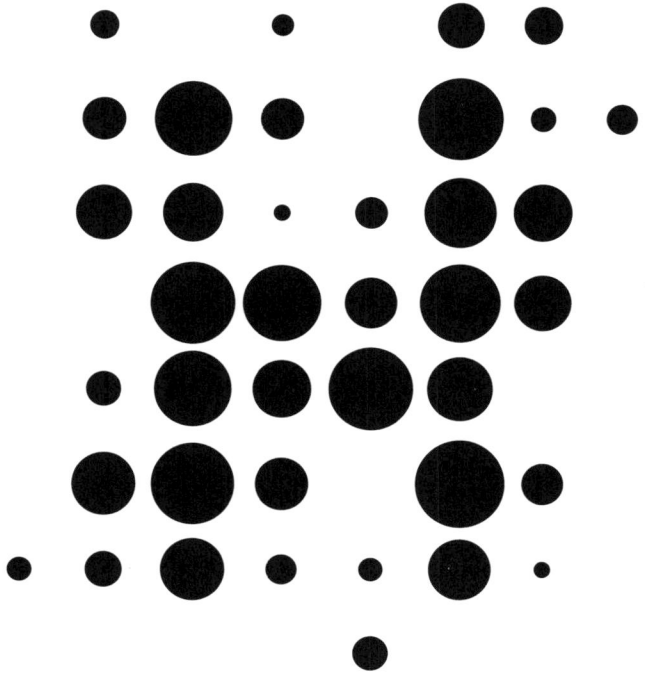

Himmelblau AG
Medical doctor

Sichtvermerk
sichtvermerk.com
Switzerland
2014

The Halcyon
Hotel

Mytton Williams
myttonwilliams.co.uk
United Kingdom
2008

Daniel Hopwood
Interior design

Two Times Elliott
2xelliott.co.uk
United Kingdom
2013

Bode-Pröve Bauunternehmen GmbH
Building contractor

Glenn Garriock
garriock.com
Germany
2013

H

Hogarth Chocolate
Chocolate maker

New Royal Standard
newroyalstandard.com
New Zealand
2013

Heraldi
Men's fashion store

Manasteriotti DS
manasteriotti.com
Croatia
2013

House
Bars & restaurants

Touch
thetouchagency.co.uk
United Kingdom
2015

H

Hazel
Personal care

Studio Mast
studiomast.co
USA
2020

Hongi
Fashion & accessories

José Design
jose-design.nl
Hong Kong, China
2013

Historic
Comprehensive beauty company

Yuta Takahashi Design Studio Co.
yutatakahashi.jp
Japan
2023

Hauforge
Animal nutrition

BRBAUEN
brbauen.com
Brazil
2016

Hanum
Law firm

BRBAUEN
brbauen.com
Brazil
2015

H

201

HYDRA.
Marketing & events

Fenton+Partners
fentonandpartners.com
United Kingdom
2009

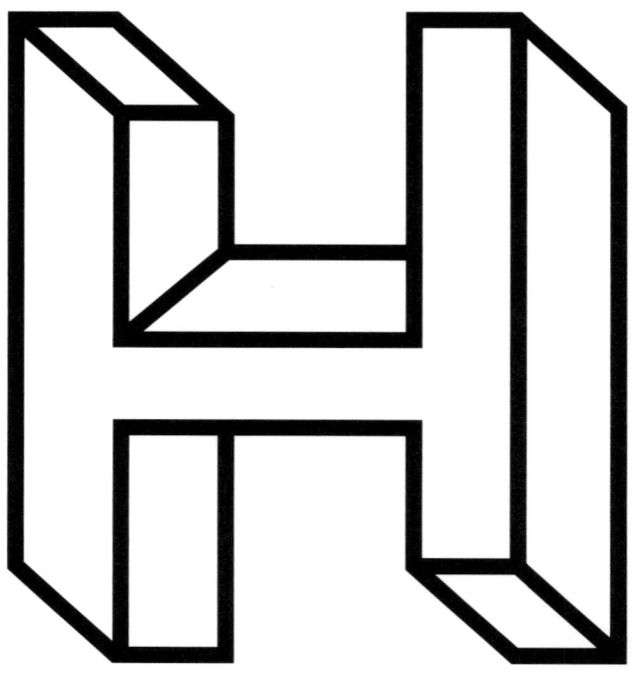

Howe Baugeschäft   H
Construction & building

Sichtvermerk
sichtvermerk.com
Germany
2007

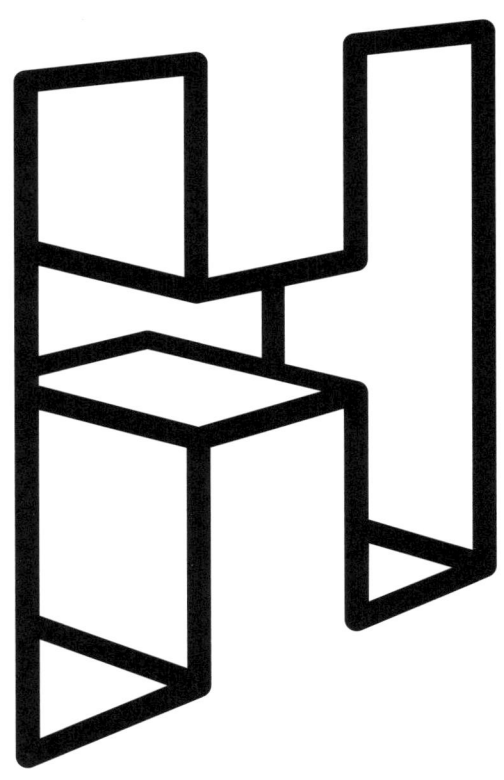

Heurtebise
Cultural association

André Covas / Inês Covas
andrecovas.com
Portugal
2015

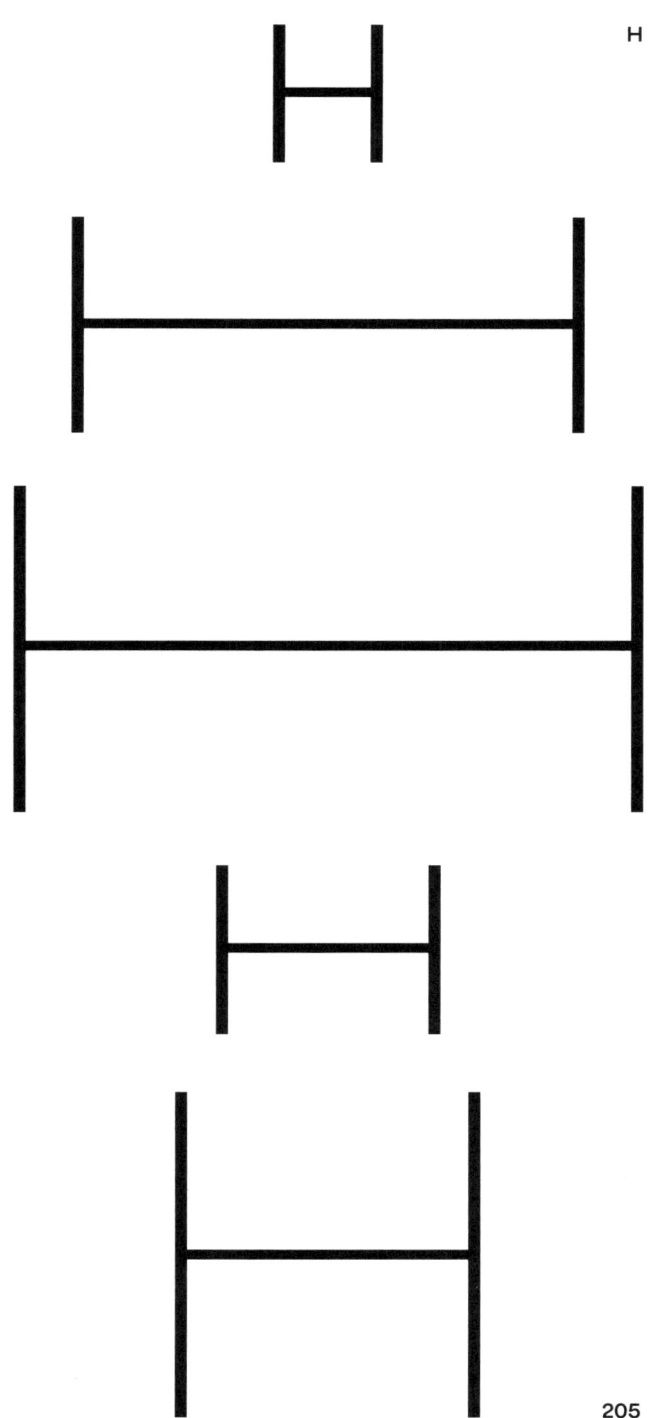

205

Horniman Museum & Gardens
Culture museum

Hat-Trick Design
hat-trickdesign.co.uk
United Kingdom
2012

Harridge Group
Travel management

Igloo
goigloo.com
United Kingdom
2013

Hazlitt
Publishers of writing on politics,
art, the environment, film, music,
sports, law & business

Monnet Design
monnet.ca
Canada
2012

H

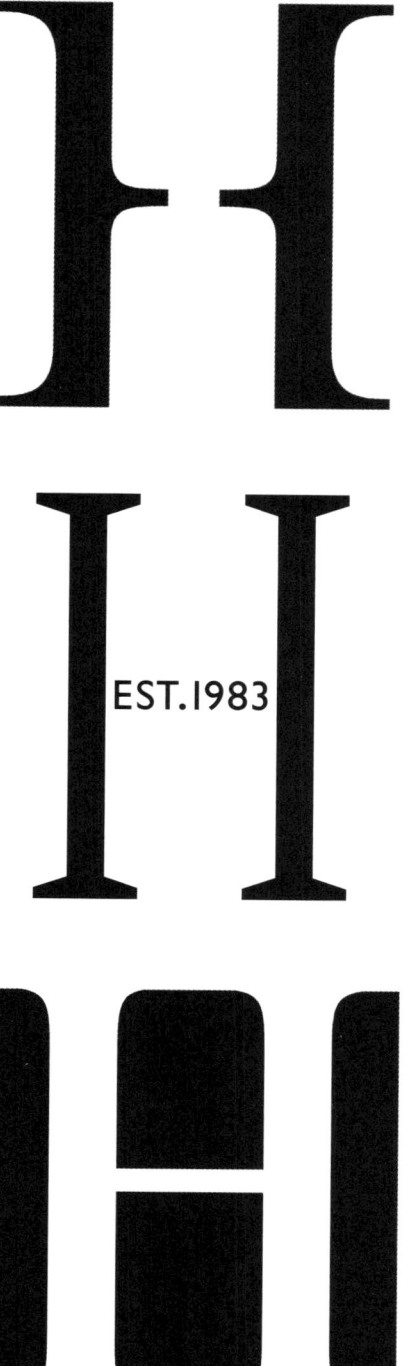

EST.1983

H Tokyo
Handkerchief shop

Donny Grafiks
donnygrafiks.com
Japan
2008

Taylore Lauren Harris
Teaching

Clarke Harris
clarkeharris.com
USA
2013

High Tea World
Website for high teas

José Design
jose-design.nl
Netherlands
2013

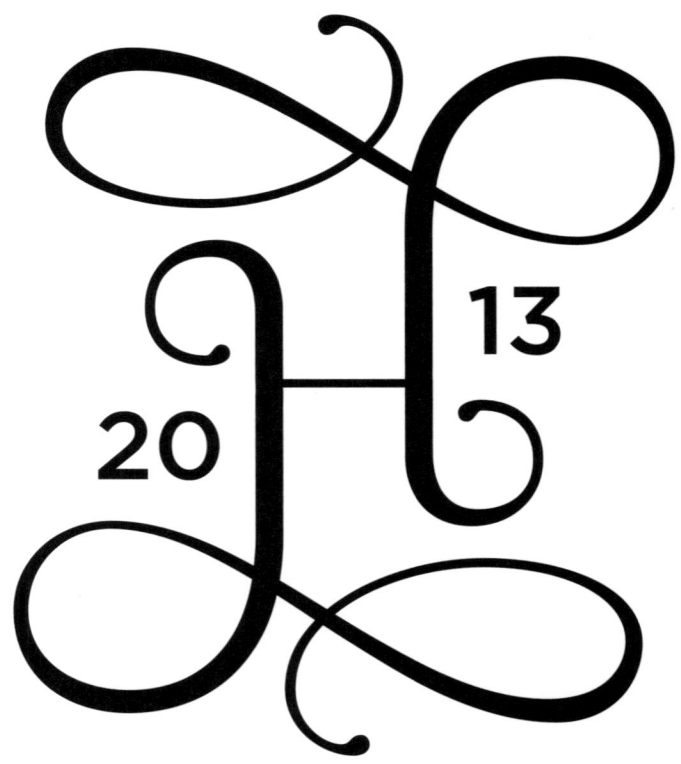

Institute of the Gut
Scientific research institute,
specialising in the gut, bowel
& stomach

The Click
theclickdesign.com
United Kingdom
2011

Join Developers
Real estate developers

La Tortillería
latortilleria.com
Mexico
2014

Judit Cabana
Translator

David de la Fuente
daviddelafuente.com
Spain
2009

IJ

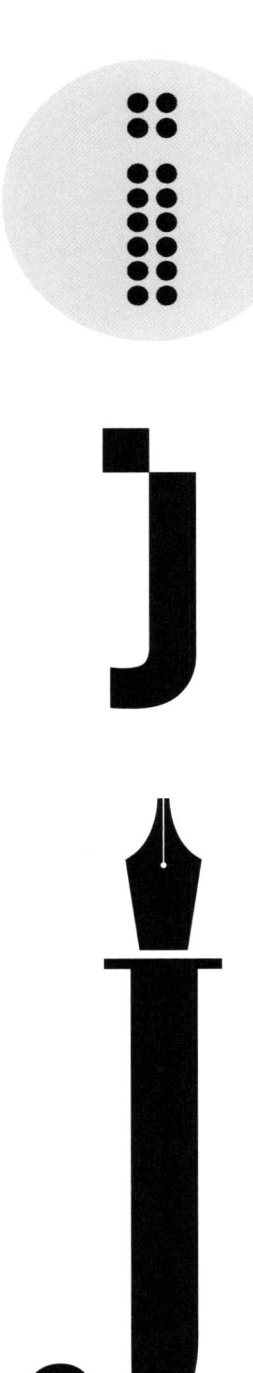

Jabberworx
Game development

Richard Baird
richardbaird.co.uk
Australia
2012

The Junction for Native
Housing development marketer

Peter & Paul
peterandpaul.co.uk
United Kingdom
2022

JPT Plumbing Services
Plumbing services

From Parts Unknown
frompartsunknown.co.uk
United Kingdom
2014

IJ

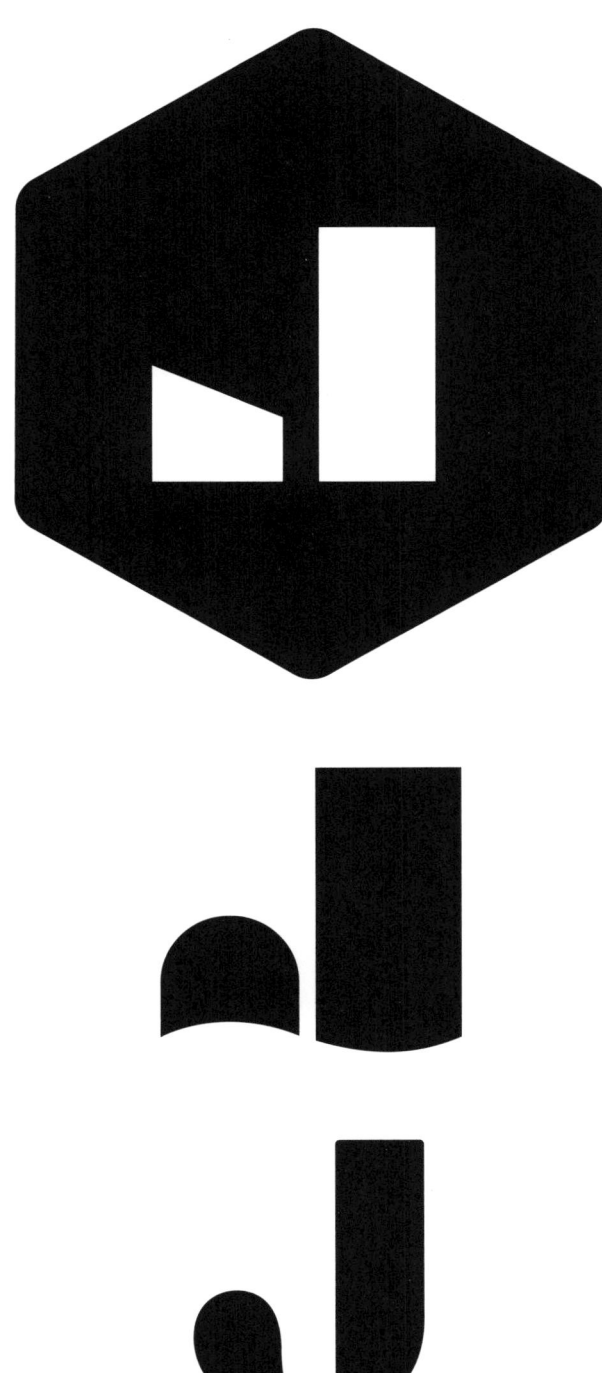

Jansky Architekturen
Architect

stapelberg&fritz
stapelbergundfritz.com
Germany
2007

Kemper Corporation
Insurance company

Lippincott
lippincott.com
USA
2011

Kickstart Media
Cross-platform media
production company

Mash Creative
mashcreative.co.uk
USA
2014

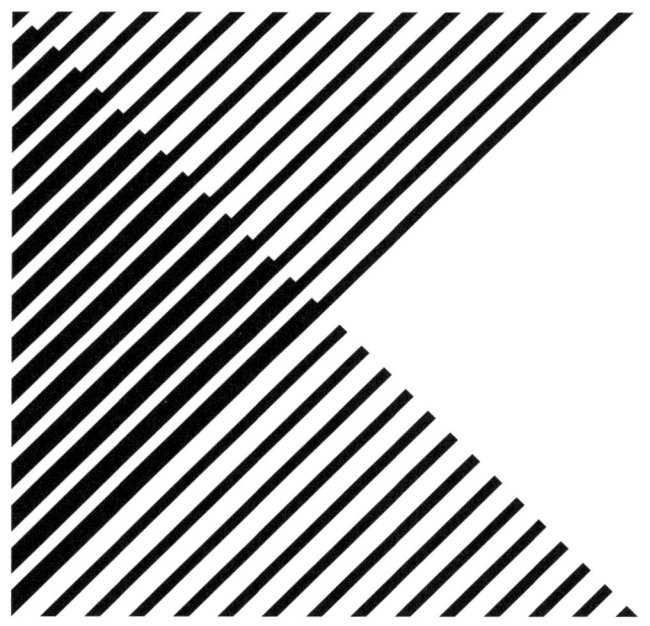

Kiyume
Men's retailer

The O Group
ogroup.net
Puerto Rico
2013

Koprina – Kazanlak
Textile factory

Stefan Kanchev
stefankanchev.com
Bulgaria
1950–1980

Laura Kriska
Cultural consulting

Foundry Collective
foundryco.com
USA
2013

Kollectiff
Web3 Agency

Berger & Föhr
bergerfohr.com
USA
2022

K

King.Dome
Real estate

Artiva Design
artiva.it
Italy
2008

Krohn
Interior architecture

Commando Group
commandogroup.no
Norway
2012

Skillcapital (internal system named Knowledgebase)
Specialist recruitment

From Parts Unknown
frompartsunknown.co.uk
United Kingdom
2013

Kitsbow
Mountain bike apparel

Manual
manualcreative.com
USA
2012

K

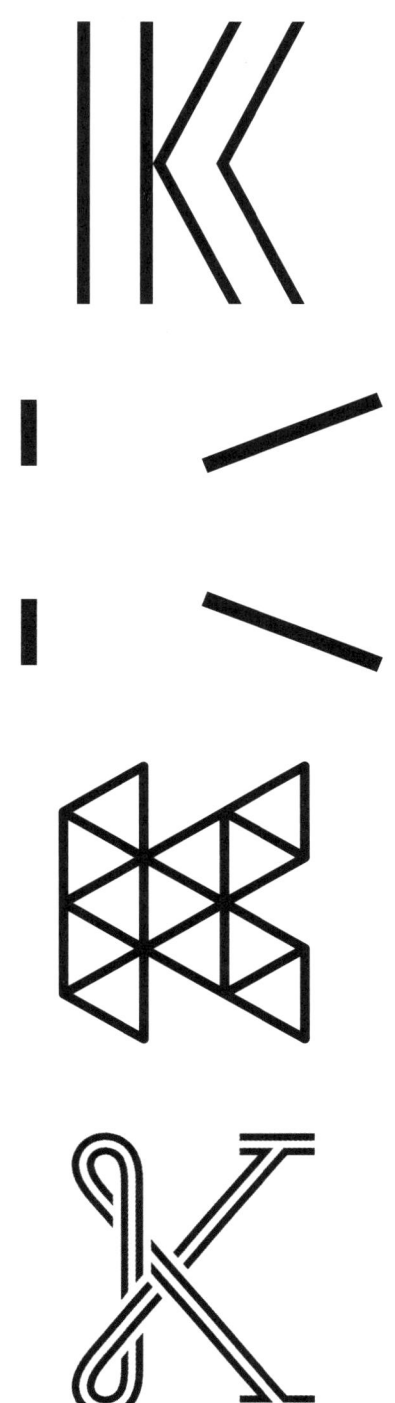

Kawabata Soushoku
Furniture

DEJIMAGRAPH Inc.
dejimagraph.com
Japan
2019

Tino Kählke
Business coaching

Büro Ink
bueroink.com
Germany
2016

Komparto
Restaurant

Chilli
Chilli.be
Belgium
2019

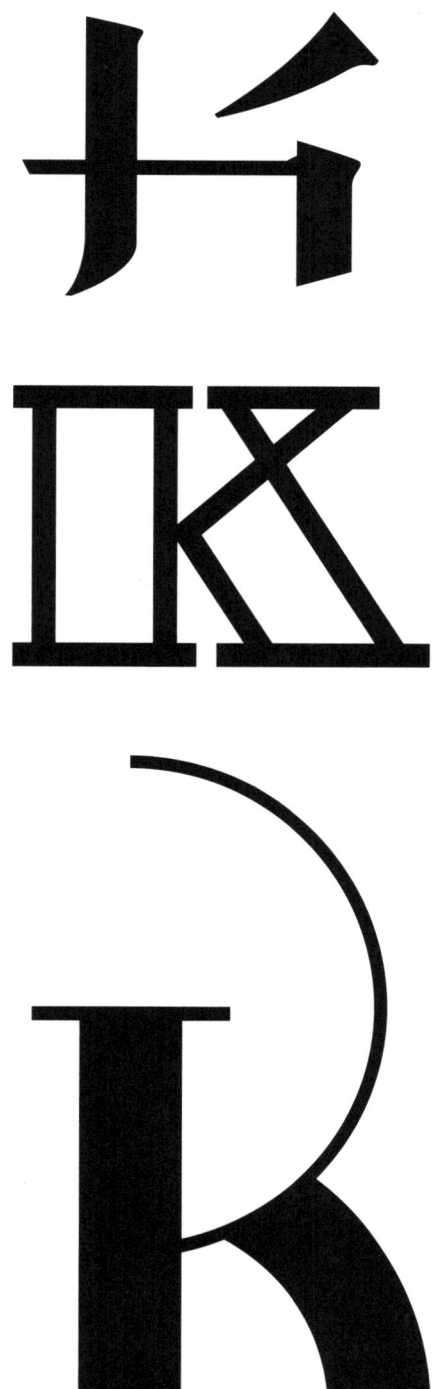

**Kings Lodge Centre
for Complex Needs**
Specialist care facility

Actual Studio
actual-studio.co.uk
United Kingdom
2014

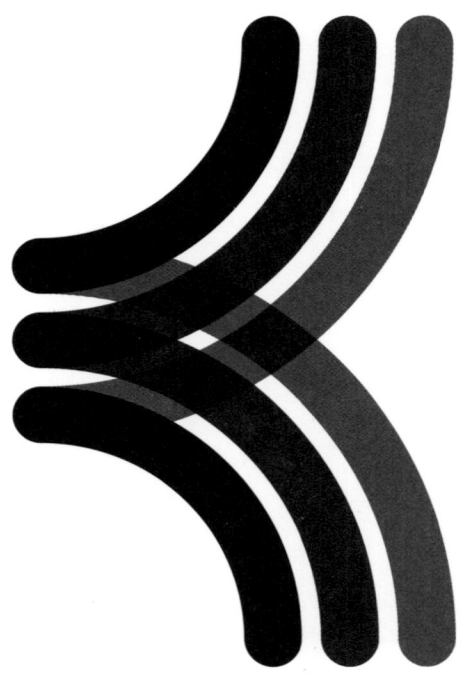

Kayla Productions
Music production

Mash Creative
mashcreative.co.uk
United Kingdom
2009

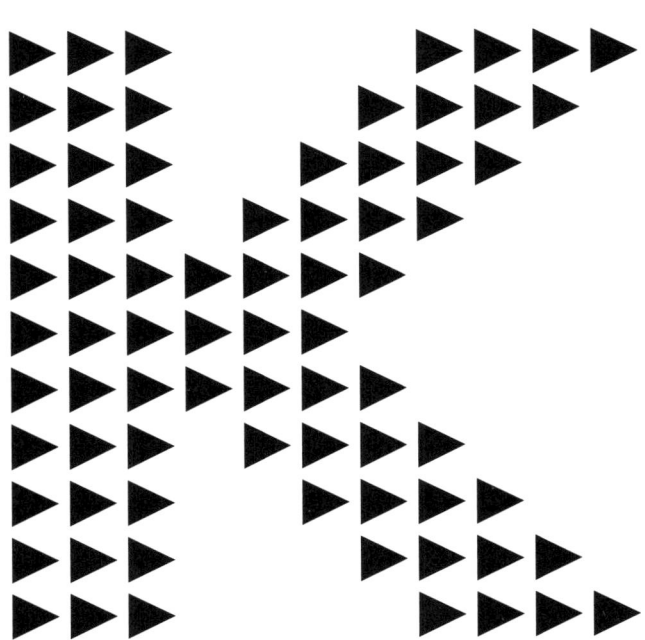

Kopec & Associates
PR services

Essex Two
sx2.com
USA
1980

Krakow Events
Event portal

Dmowski & Co.
dmowski.co
Poland
2012

Keystone Capital
Investment

SocioDesign
sociodesign.co.uk
France
2014

Kallen Engineering
Manufacturer & supplier
of bit grinding systems

Believe in®
believein.co.uk
United Kingdom
2005

K

The Knot
All-in-one wedding planning

Koto
koto.studio
USA
2023

Komma
Publisher

Design by Toko
designbytoko.com
The Netherlands
2022

Kingdom
Pet products

BRBAUEN
brbauen.com
Brazil
2019

K

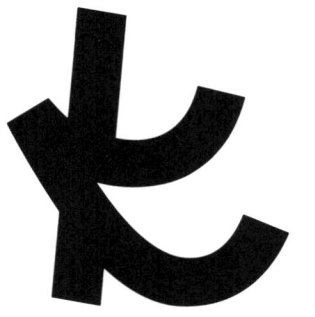

K2LD Architects
Architects

Studio Hi Ho
studiohiho.com
Australia
2012

Kontion Saha
Sawmill

Kari Piippo
piippo.com/kari
Finland
1984

**Kansallinen Lääkeinform-
aatiokeskus Klik Oy**
Medicine & drug information centre

Hahmo Design Ltd.
hahmo.fi
Finland
2012

KALAS Sportswear, s.r.o.
Manufacturer of custom cycling clothes

Studio Echt
studioecht.com
Slovakia
2019

K

233

Kitamura
Cameras

6D
6d-k.com
Japan
2020

Studio Kontus
Photography

Manasteriotti DS
manasteriotti.com
Croatia
2014

K

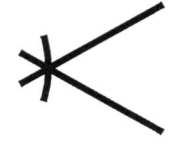

北村写真機店

Kitamura Camera

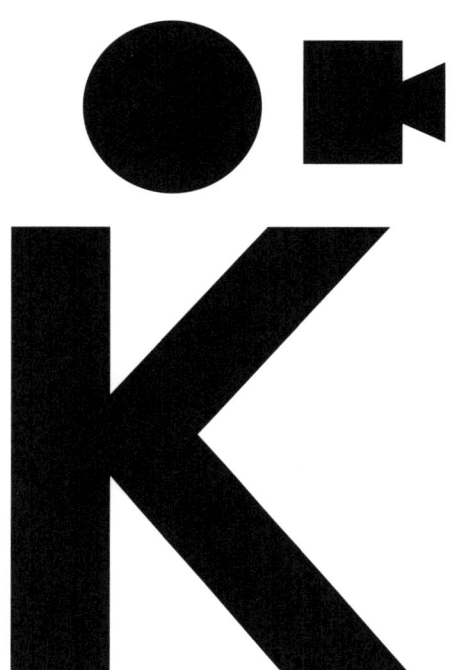

Karin de Riszner
College entrance consultancy

Corey Holms
coreyholms.com
USA
2004

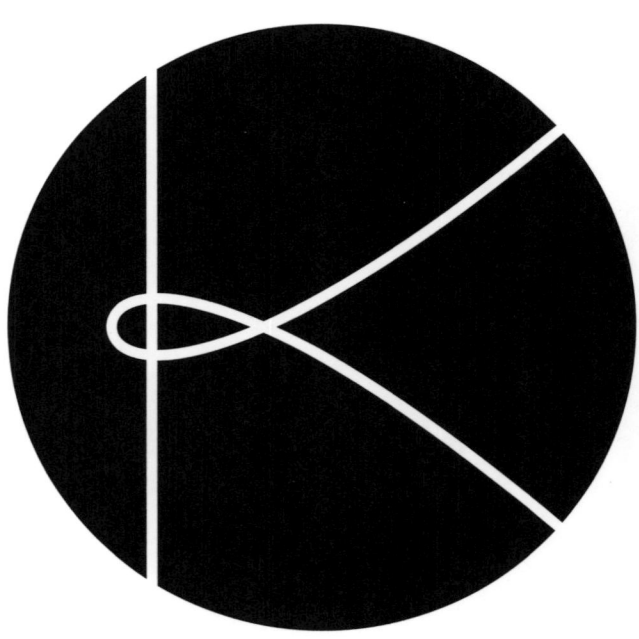

Kreative Oslo
Organisation working for
Oslo's cultural industries

Nicklas Haslestad
nicklashaslestad.com
Norway
2013

K

Kudo Solutions
Website design & development

Buddy Creative
buddycreative.com
United Kingdom
2010

Kalideen Acupuncture
Acupuncturist

Magpie Studio
magpie-studio.com
United Kingdom
2008

Kitbag.com
Online fanwear retailers

Studio Contents commissioned
by Photolink Creative Group
studiocontents.com
United Kingdom
2012

Colours of the Kalahari
Exhibition of Southern African
bushman art

Believe in®
believein.co.uk
United Kingdom
2013

K

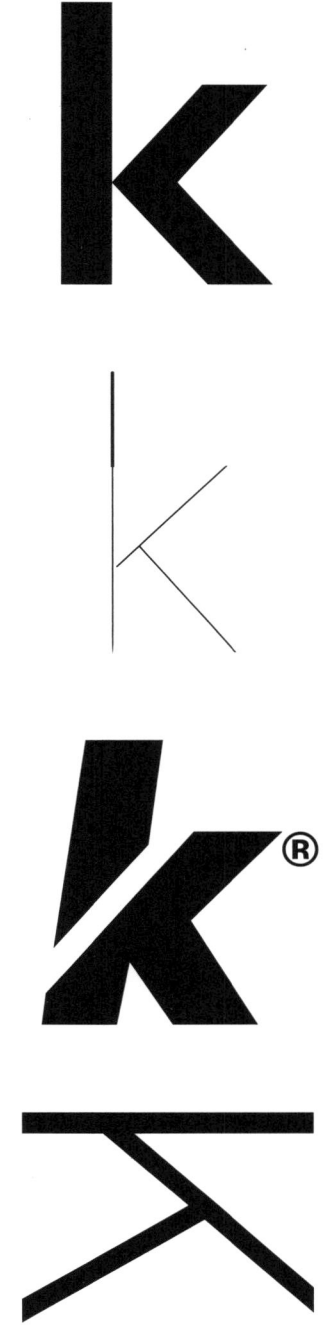

Knights Paving & Landscaping
Paving & landscaping

JB Studio
jb-studio.co.uk
United Kingdom
2015

Kingston Cultural Area, Norfolk Island
World heritage site

K

Pidgeon Ward
pidgeonward.com.au
Australia
2020

The Keys
Property development

Rob Clarke Type Design & Lettering /
Rareform
robclarke.com
United Kingdom
2007

Bodega & Viñedos Korta Bucarey
Winery

Ole Büro
oleburo.com
Chile
2014

**Kentucky Music Hall of Fame
and Museum**
Museum honouring native
Kentucky music professionals

Malcolm Grear Designers
mgrear.com
USA
1999

Kaori Hair Studio
Hair stylist

Gee + Chung Design
geechungdesign.com
USA
2013

L

Tesoro Publico Letras
Spanish public treasury

Cruz Novillo
cruznovillo.com
Spain
1984

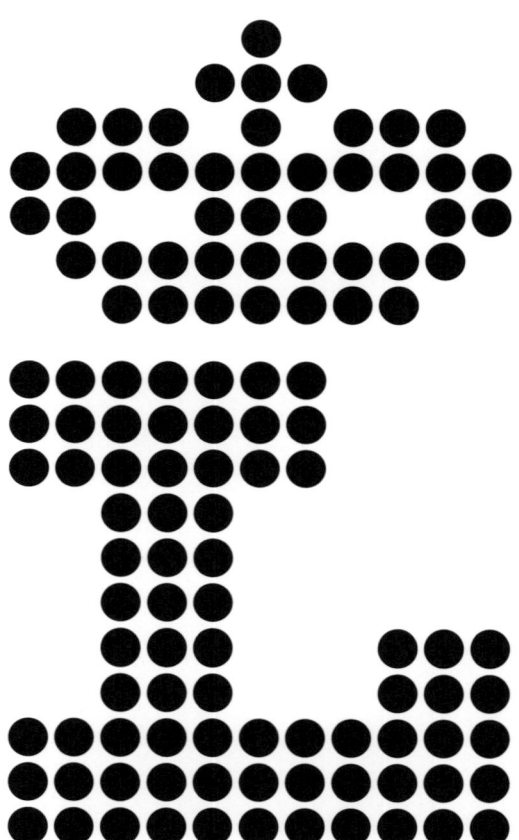

Lift London L
Software development

New Royal Standard
newroyalstandard.com
United Kingdom
2013

Ladler
Producing & selling curling stones

Lukas Diemling
diemling.com
Austria
2022

Lifthing
An industrial installation company

Chilli
Chilli.be
Belgium
2015

Lotus Ultrasonic Scalpels
Health care

Mytton Williams
myttonwilliams.co.uk
United Kingdom
2011

L

Liane Yumi Ikemoto
Art conservator

Scott Naauao
naauao.com
USA
2012

Liptrot Illustration
Illustration

Mike Scott / MGS
mike-scott.co.uk
United Kingdom
2014

L

Liberating IT
Digital development agency

From Parts Unknown
frompartsunknown.co.uk
United Kingdom
2014

L

Lanpro
Multi-disciplinary planning consultancy

The Click
theclickdesign.com
United Kingdom
2024

M

Mattis Erngren
Project management

1910 Design & Communication
weare1910.com
Sweden
2012

Manufactum Concept Store
Fashion retail

Bienal Comunicación
bienal.mx
Mexico
2012

Millby Foundation
Charity

Magpie Studio
magpie-studio.com
United Kingdom
2012

Patrick Beaulieu
Visual artist

Feed
studiofeed.ca
Canada
2014

M

Musiikkitalo – Helsinki Music Centre
Concert venue & meeting place

Hahmo Design Oy
hahmo.fi
Finland
2007

Meubles.comn / Groupe Matelsom
Furniture retailer

FL@33
flat33.com
France
2003

Mary Oh
Lingerie boutique

Face
designbyface.com
Germany
2011

M

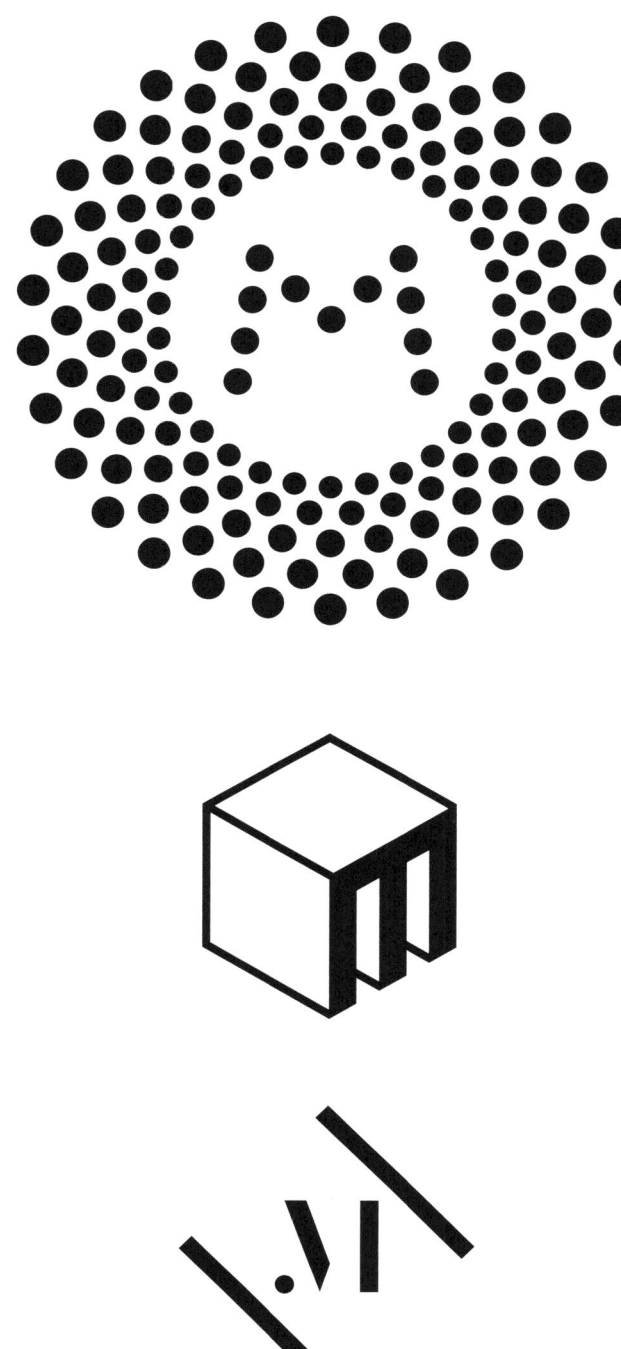

Mvstard
E-commerce platform

Think Work Observe
t-wo.it
United Kingdom
2013

MileIQ
Milage tracker app

Strohl
strohlsf.com
USA
2013

Mashinoimport
Import company

Stefan Kanchev
stefankanchev.com
Bulgaria
1950–1980

Mendes Junior
Steel manufacturing & global construction

Richard Danne & Associates
dannedesign.com
Brazil
1994

M

Mingazzini e Figli
Cardboard manufacturer

Maurizio Milani
milanidesign.it
Italy
1977

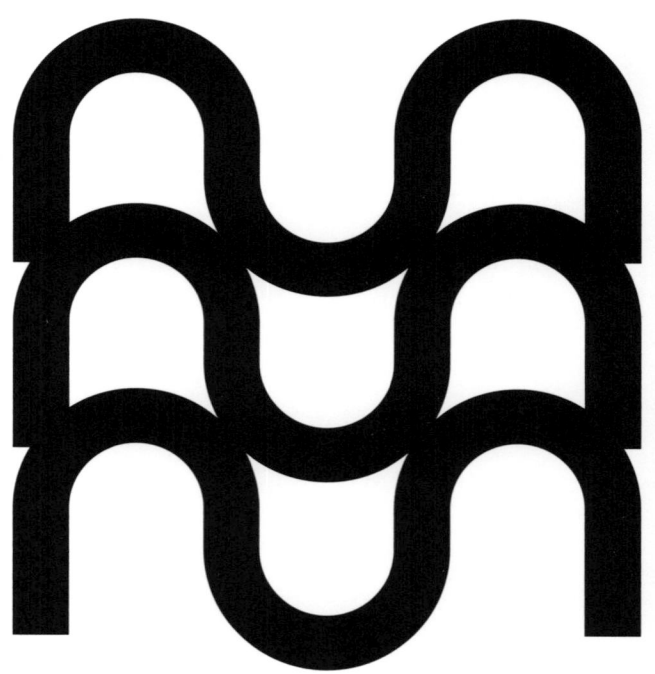

Morphic M
Scan-3D-print technology

Berger & Föhr
bergerfohr.com
USA
2020

Marcel Lehmann
Gardening company

Studio Eusebio
studioeusebio.com
Switzerland
2014

Maker Projects
Creative production company
making short films, branded
content & music videos

Studio Contents
studiocontents.com
United Kingdom
2013

Construcciones Mecanizadas
Road & way building with
prefabricated modules

diseñollosa
diseñollosa.com.ar
Argentina / Latin America
Circa 1980

Modern Shows
Organisers of shows of midcentury
and contemporary furniture & design

Hyperkit
hyperkit.co.uk
United Kingdom
2011

M

MainStreet
Fintech

What Else Studio
whatelse.studio
USA
2022

Mito Media
Video production company

Berger & Föhr
bergerfohr.com
USA
2009

Mean
Audio software & hardware

Give Up Art
giveupart.com
New Zealand
2013

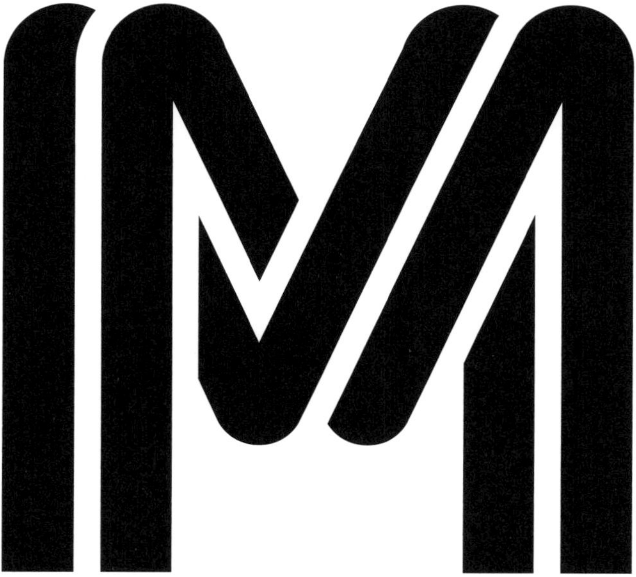

M

Mme KIKI
Sweet shop

UMA / design farm
umamu.jp
Japan
2012

Motion Music
Tour management company

Face
designbyface.com
USA
2013

Morpheus Homes
Property developers

JB Studio
jordanblyth.com
United Kingdom
2012

MIDAS (Manchester Business Clubs)
Inward investment agency

From Parts Unknown
frompartsunknown.co.uk
United Kingdom
2010

M

Mme KIKI

Molino Rojo
Peruvian rice brand

Brandlab
brandlab.pe
Peru
2013

Megabite
Big game fishing charter

M

Manasteriotti DS
manasteriotti.com
Croatia
2012

Mentres
Building company

Chilli
chilli.be
Belgium
2014

Mahabis
Footwear

IYA Studio
iyastudio.co.uk
United Kingdom
2014

Ilkka Marttiini Oy
High quality steel products

Hahmo Design Oy
hahmo.fi
Finland
2007

Monir Jewellery
Jewellery

Studio Es
studio-es.at
Austria
2012

M

M Gallery
Luxury hotels

W&cie
wcie.fr
France
2008

Maison Girardin
International artist residency program

Feed
studiofeed.ca
Canada
2012

Mathieu Gustafsson Design
Furniture designer

Ateljé Altmann
ateljealtmann.com
Sweden
2011

Metyis
Strategy & execution

Metyis Design Studio
metyis.com
Global
2021

Marazul / Ajuntament de Valencia
Cultural center

Opisso Studio
opissostudio.com
Spain
2012

Mercury Payment Systems
Point-of-sale systems that simplify
payment processing solutions

Brick Design
bricksf.com
USA
2012

Manto
Concept shop

DEJIMAGRAPH Inc.
dejimagraph.com
Japan
2014

Minimo
Contemporary furniture retailer

Two
twodesign.co.uk
United Kingdom
2006

Modterra
Construction

Studio Mast
studiomast.co
USA
2018

M

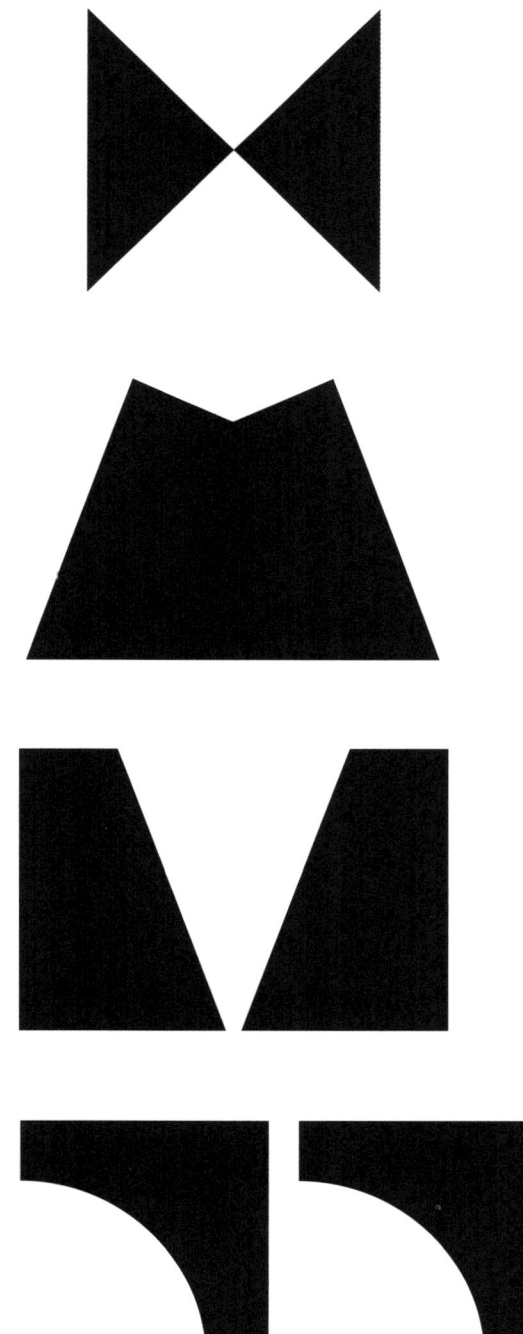

Valenta Mangagement
Culture & artist management

Studio Es
studio-es.at
Austria
2014

Montrose
Fashion

Canefantasma
canefantasma.com
United Kingdom
2015

Marzipan
Marzipan music

stapelberg&fritz
stapelbergundfritz.com
Germany
2007

Manufactura Textil Patagónica
Manufacturer of woven fabrics
of synthetic fibers

diseñollosa
diseñollosa.com.ar
Multinational
Circa 2000

Girl Meet Money (GMM)
Female-led fintech company

Blok Design
blokdesign.com
Canada
2022

M

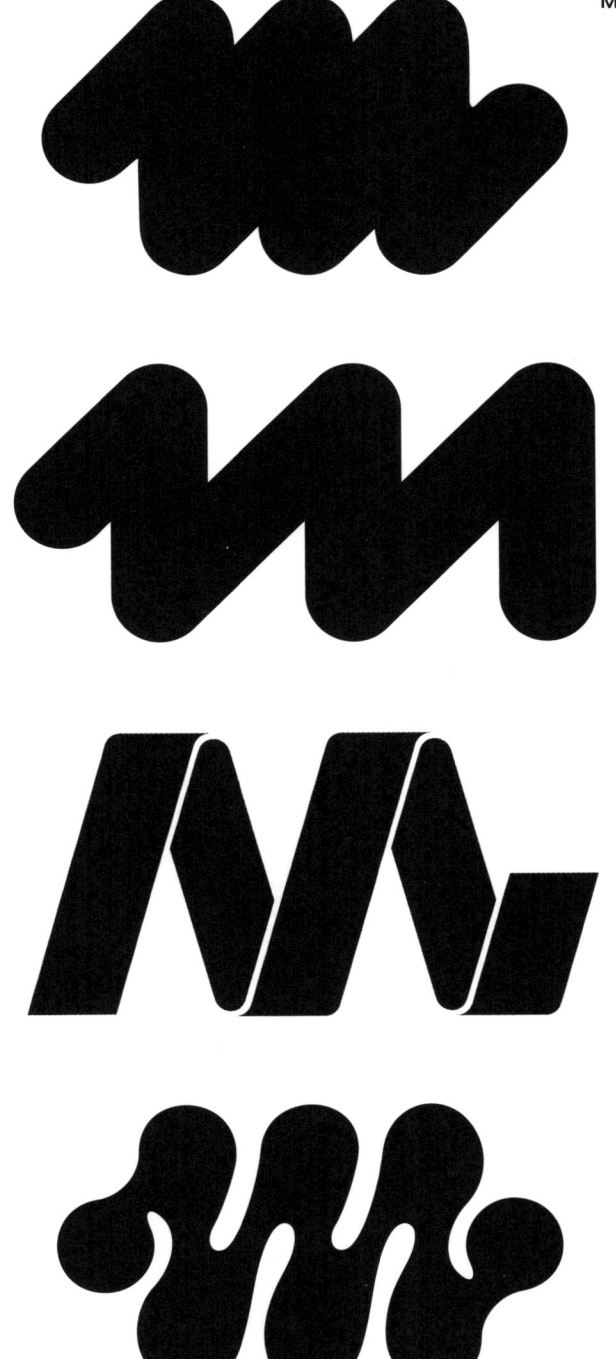

Fundación C.R.D.O. Montes de Toledo
Oil protected designation of origin

Aitor Baigorri
aitorbaigorri.com
Spain
2018

The Mountain Company
Adventure travel company

Ragged Edge
raggededge.com
United Kingdom
2009

My Value
Open banking solutions

Sonia Castillo Studio
soniacastillo.com
Spain
2020

Malina Kostenets
Peronal mark

Stefan Kanchev
stefankanchev.com
Bulgaria
1958

M

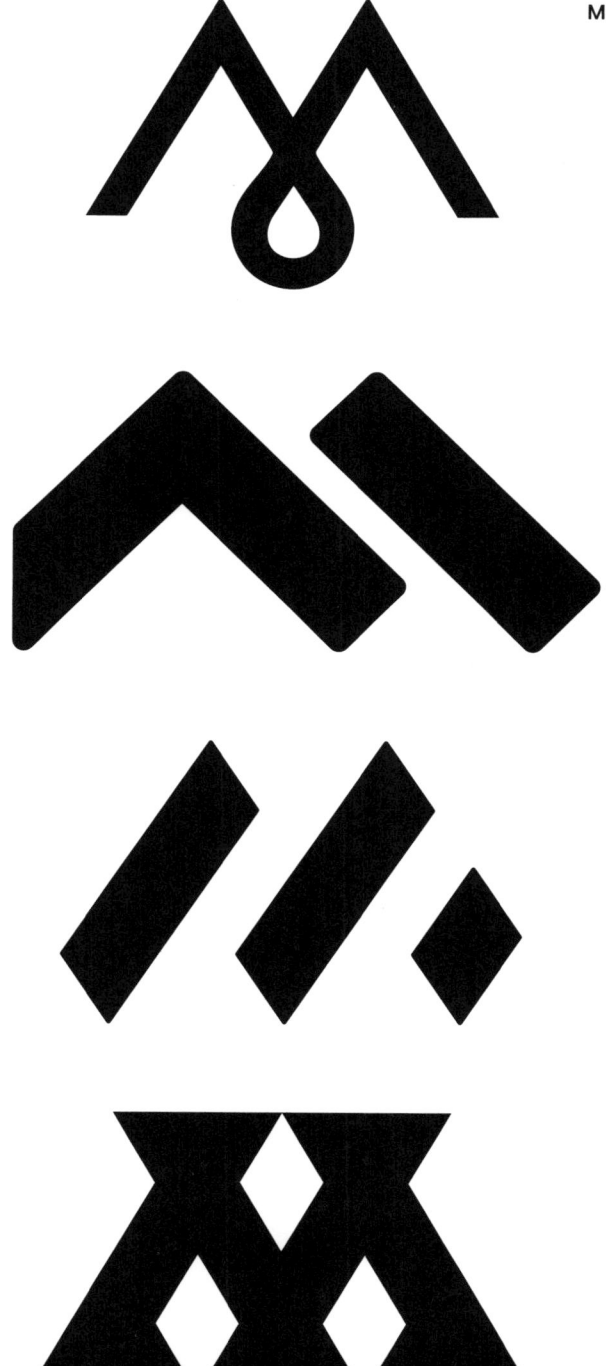

285

Milton Agency
Talent agency for hair and
make-up artists & costume
designers

Magpie Studio
magpie-studio.com
United Kingdom
2009

Madrid
Community of Madrid

Cruz Novillo
cruznovillo.com
Spain
1985

Mallowpuffs
Vegan marshmallows

Midday
middaystudio.com
Belgium
2018

Manbuloo
Mango grower

inkahoots
inkahoots.com.au
Australia
2006

Andrew Mathiot
Music DJ

Mash Creative
mashcreative.co.uk
United Kingdom
2009

M

Preciz-Michai
Metals

Stefan Kanchev
stefankanchev.com
Bulgaria
1972

Muzik School of Creation and Production
Independent school for music creation & production

Oded Ezer Typography
odedezer.com
Israel
2005

Meridian
Premium grooming solutions

Koto
koto.studio
USA
2022

Momentum
Pilates studio

P.A.R
p-a-r.net
Mexico
2012

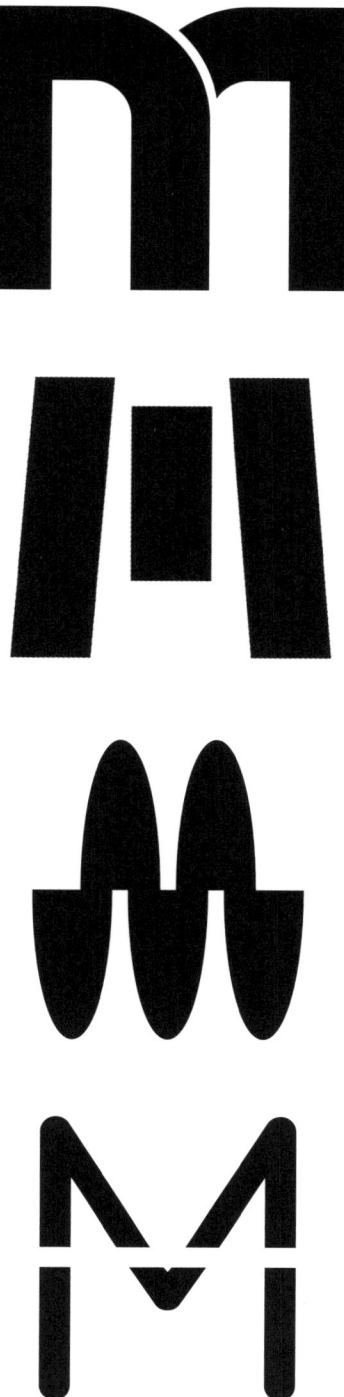

M

291

Murmure
Creative agency

Murmure
murmure.me
France
2012

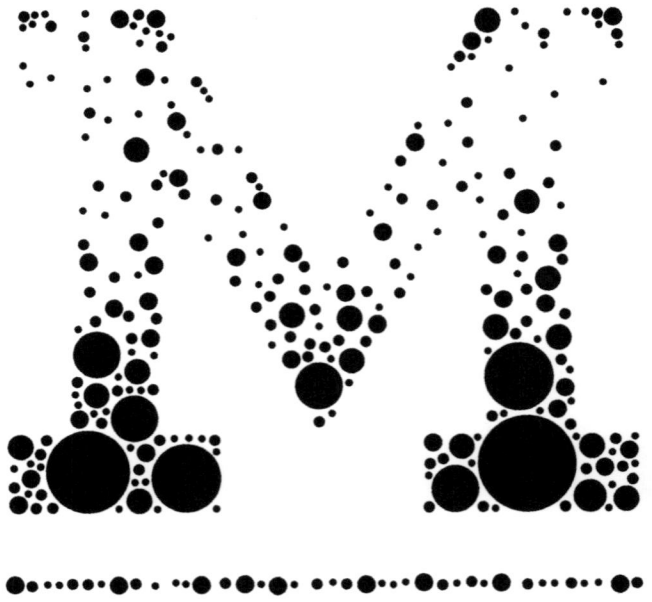

Nowicki
Lawyer

Dmowski & Co.
dmowski.co
Poland
2014

NIDA
National Institute of Dramatic Art

Maud
maud.com.au
Australia
2014

Nemo TV
Interactive TV

Brandberry
brandberry.net
United Kingdom
2013

Nasca Kitchen
Peruvian restaurant

Tractorbeam
tractorbeam.com
USA
2012

Nichols Consultancy
Global headhunters

Kimpton Creative
kimptoncreative.com
United Kingdom
2009

New North
Nitro coffee

Campbell Hay
campbellhay.com
United Kingdom
2017

Nothnagle Realtors
Realty firm

Kyle O'Hara Design
kyleohara.com
USA
2010

Newman Properties
Property and land investors
& developers

K Art and Design, Inc.
k-artanddesign.com
USA
2009

Netconnect
Internet provider

Büro Ink
bueroink.com
Switzerland
2021

N

The Department of No
Art & design research

Andy Lang / Craig Sinnamon
nullzero.studio
United Kingdom
2013

L' atelier Nivernais
Handmade potteries & house decoration

José Design
jose-design.nl
Taipei, China
2013

The Nth Degree Club
Exclusive private dining club

Ragged Edge
raggededge.com
United Kingdom
2010

N

Nanocosm Technologies
Internet commerce

Gee + Chung Design
geechungdesign.com
USA
1998

Nexus
Finance

Studio Mast
studiomast.co
USA
2022

Nicola Tilling
Marketing services

Mytton Williams
myttonwilliams.co.uk
United Kingdom
2007

Nutmeg Films
Film production

Ascend Studio
ascendstudio.co.uk
United Kingdom
2022

N

Nextbus
Real-time transit GPS

Nancy Wu Design
nancywudesign.com
Canada
2010

Nertal
Construction company

Cruz Novillo
cruznovillo.com
Spain
1966

National Centre for Writing
The UK's national body for
literature and hub for writers

The Click
theclickdesign.com
United Kingdom
2018

River North Association
Community business association

Essex Two
sx2.com
USA
2003

Nordiq Energy
Energy usage consultancy

Add Studio
addstudio.se
Sweden
2020

Nomo
Telecom

BRBAUEN
brbauen.com
Brazil
2022

Província
Real estate developments

BRBAUEN
brbauen.com
Brazil
2020

N

Nephila
Investment manager specialising
in catastrophe reinsurance risk

Coley Porter Bell
coleyporterbell.com
UK / USA
2019

Neill
Legacy hair & beauty holding company

High Tide
hightidenyc.com
USA
2022

North Collective
Brand strategy

Freytag Anderson
freytaganderson.com
United Kingdom
2013

The Ninetys
Music production

Anton Burmistrov
antonburmistrov.com
United Kingdom
2013

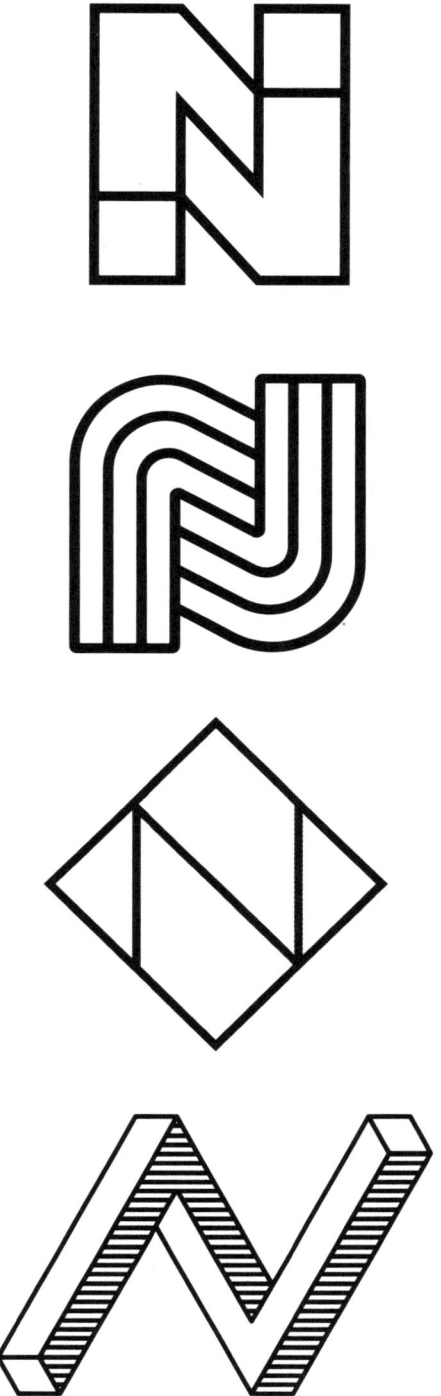
N

NEPTCO
New England printed tape company

Malcolm Grear Designers
mgrear.com
USA
1978

Ob-Sessions
Broadcasting

Quim Marin
quimmarin.com
Spain
2012

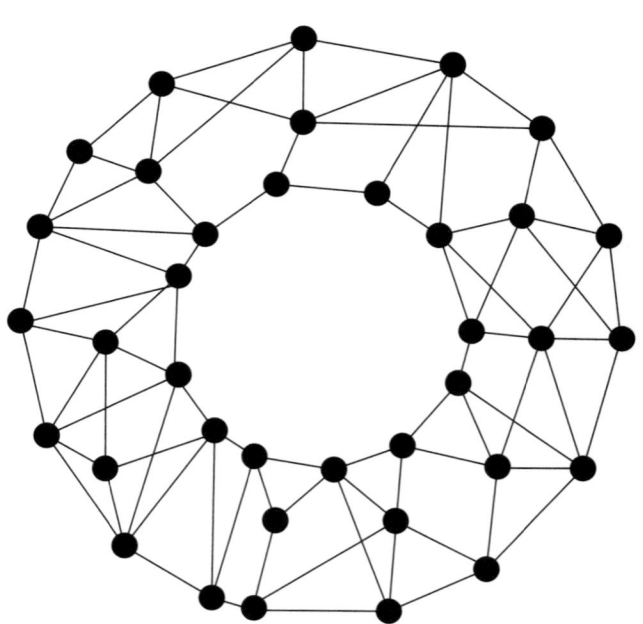

'O' New Media
Digital advertising technology company

Mash Creative
mashcreative.co.uk
United Kingdom
2011

O

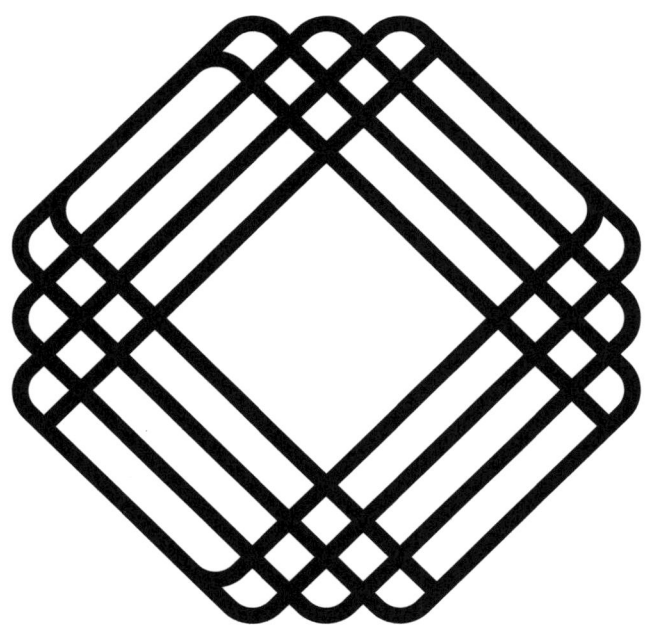

Orains
Interior design products made
with local wool from the west
coast of Scotland

my:creative
thisismycreative.com
United Kingdom / Netherlands
2014

Onyx
Recruitment

Mash Creative
mashcreative.co.uk
United Kingdom
2010

The One Centre
Brand transmedia agency

Moffitt.Moffitt.
moffittmoffitt.com
Australia
2012

Olive Management Solutions
Business management solutions

Richard Baird
richardbaird.co.uk
United Kingdom
2010

o

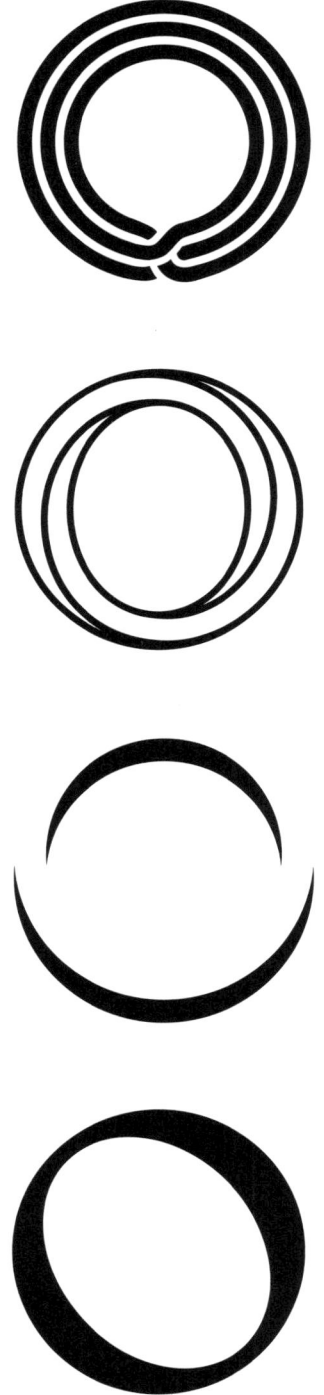

Oprah Winfrey
Entertainer

Essex Two
sx2.com
USA
1989

Optimalé
Health centre

Chilli
chilli.be
Belgium
2012

Extravirgen Olive Oil Store
Olive oil store

Ángel Plaza
angel-plaza.com
Spain
2013

Opine Experts
Legal resource providing expert opinions & consultation for real estate issues

Brick Design
bricksf.com
USA
2011

o

317

Oldawan
Healthy café

SocioDesign
sociodesign.co.uk
USA
2014

O2
Telecommunications

Lambie-Nairn
lambie-nairn.com
Global
2002

Optimalé
Health centre

Chilli
chilli.be
Belgium
2012

Mikkelin Kaupungin Orkesteri
Music orchestra

Kari Piippo
piippo.com/kari
Finland
2000

o

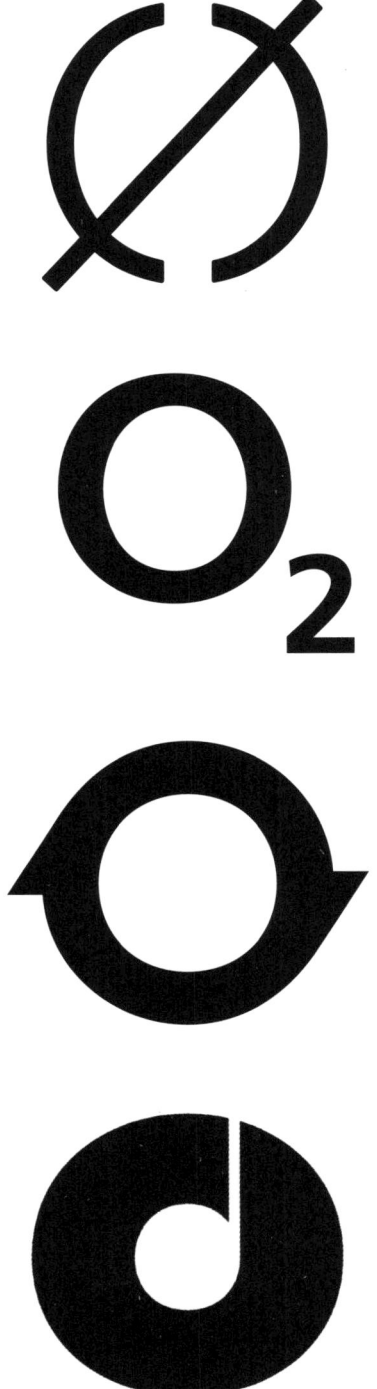

ZEROawards for UNICEF
Children's fund

Rice Creative
rice-creative.com
USA
2013

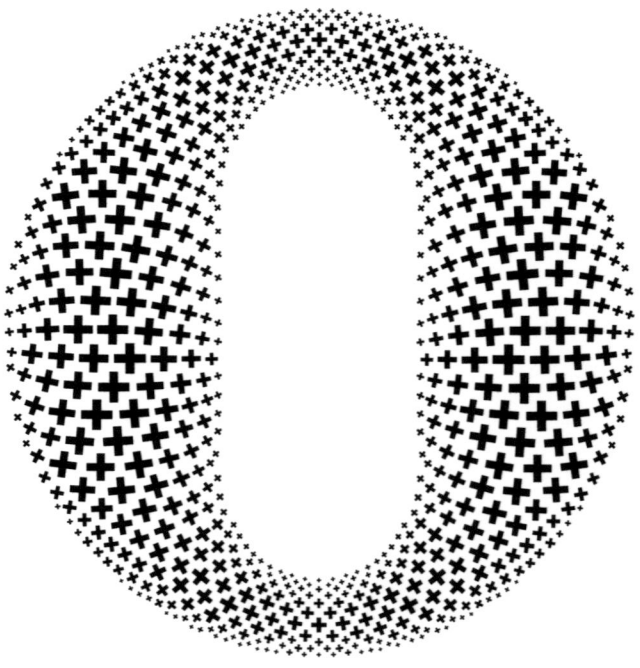

Framepage / Hanna Raijas
Photographer

Hahmo Design Oy
hahmo.fi
Finland
2009

Proesur
Construction & architecture

Bienal Comunicación
bienal.mx
Mexico
2013

Self-intitiated

Duane Dalton
duanedalton.com
Ireland
2014

POS+
Mobile POS services

6D
6d-k.com
Japan
2019

P

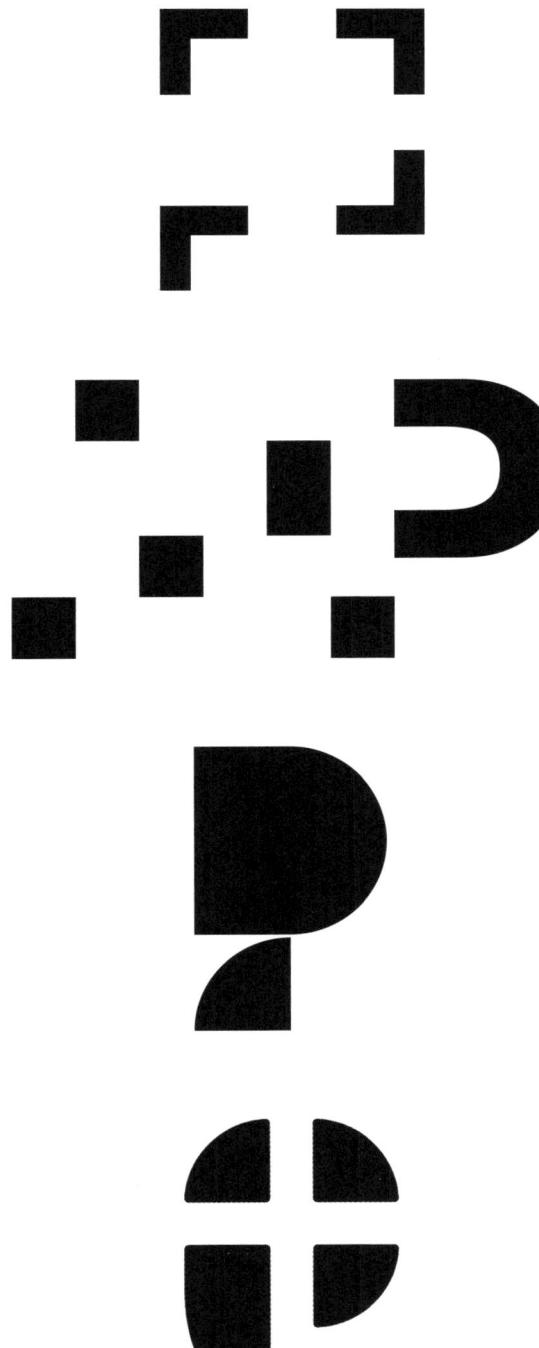

Palapita
Online store selling storage solutions

Carlos Galán Rubio
galanrubio.com
Spain
2016

Proven
Restaurant job app

Strohl
strohlsf.com
USA
2013

Pacsa
Construction company

Cruz Novillo
cruznovillo.com
Spain
1992

Sala Paternak
Live music club

Quim Marin
quimmarin.com
Spain
2014

P

PlusFloor
Flooring solutions

Freytag Anderson
freytaganderson.com
United Kingdom
2023

Parser
IT

Pedro Paulino
pedropaulino.com
Brazil
2014

Phi
Builder & real estate

üla
ula.com.ar
Argentina
2023

InterPark International
Parking & garage services

Essex Two
sx2.com
USA
2000

P

Plener (Open air)
Outdoor night club

Dmowski&Co.
dmowski.co
Poland
2015

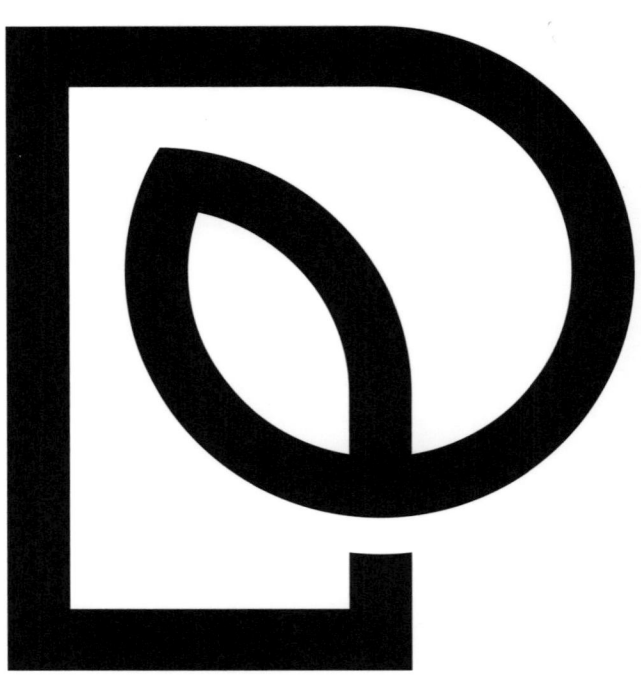

Pursuit
Non-profit

Gander
takeagander.com
USA
2018

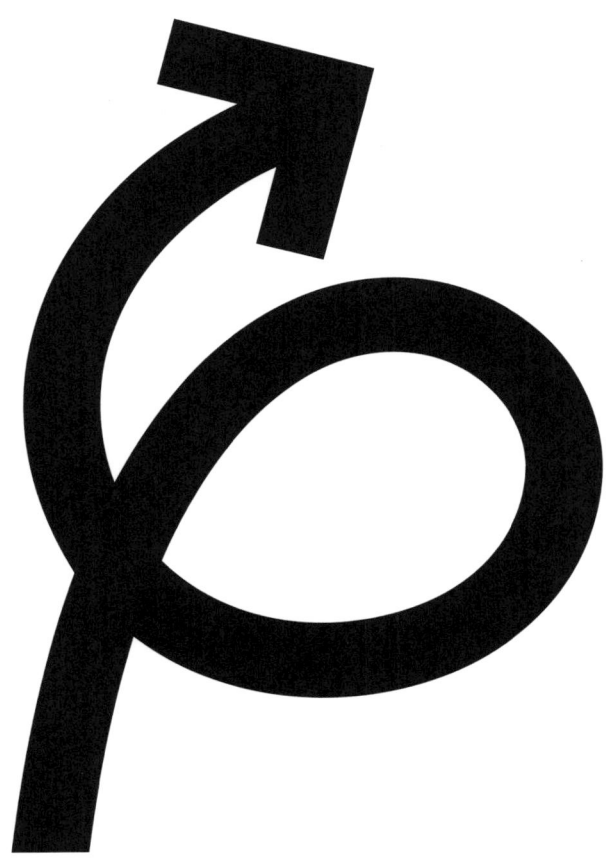

Pushworks
Integrated marketing solutions

From Parts Unknown
frompartsunknown.co.uk
United Kingdom
2011

Psychonaut
Publishing

Abby Haddican Studio
abbyhaddican.com
USA
2021

Peache
A storytelling and production
studio for travel & hospitality

After Hours
afterhoursstudio.com.au
London
2022

Parc Architecture
Architecture

Müesli
ateliermuesli.com
France
2009

P

Press Green
Printers

From Parts Unknown
frompartsunknown.co.uk
United Kingdom
2012

Paquexpres
Railway shipping of packages

Cruz Novillo
cruznovillo.com
Spain
1990

Pirongs
Diaries & planners for education

Mytton Williams
myttonwilliams.co.uk
United Kingdom
2013

Prodigi
Print on demand

Freytag Anderson
freytaganderson.com
United Kingdom
2019

P

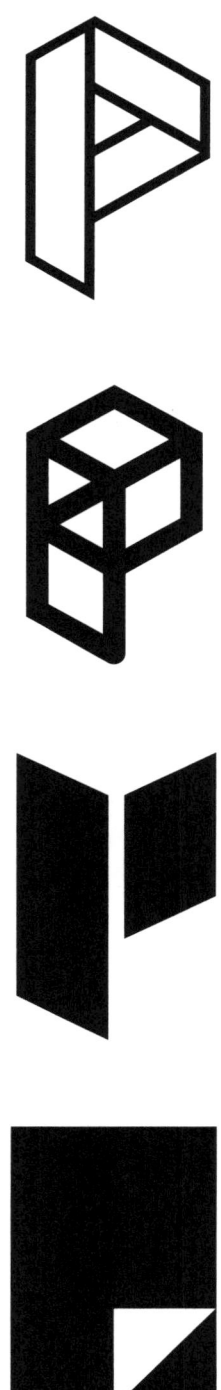

Pholium
App for creating a photography book

Six
madebysix.com
USA
2012

The Punch Project
Studio, gallery & shop

I See Sea
iseesea.co.uk
United Kingdom
2014

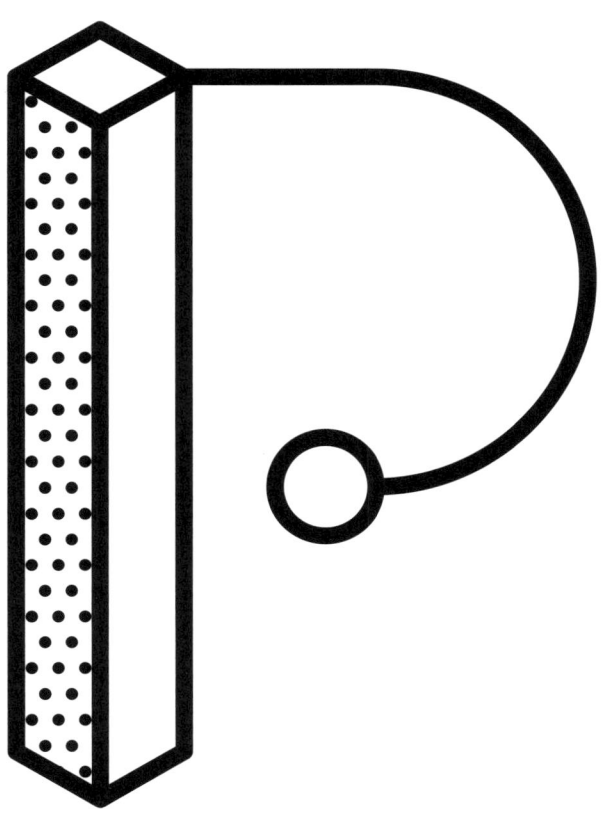

Praga
Hair salon

invade
invade.design
Colombia
2022

Pintaudi
Cakes & biscuits

Matteo Bartoli – Graphic Design Studio
matteobartoli.com
Italy
2012

Publisha
Online publishing platform

Leterme Dowling
letermedowling.com
United Kingdom
2010

Pronto Light
Food

Pedro Paulino
pedropaulino.com
Brazil
2014

P

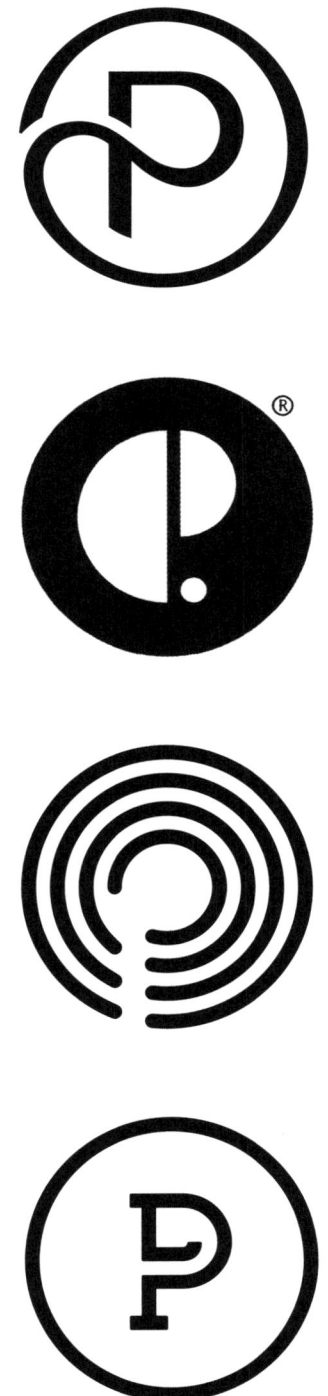

Fundación Peruana del Cancer
Nonprofit entity raising funds
to fight childhood cancer

Brandlab
brandlab.pe
Peru
2009

Pochle
Distilled apple spirit

Freytag Anderson
freytaganderson.com
United Kingdom
2023

Pensthorpe
Nature reserve & visitor attraction

The Click
theclickdesign.com
United Kingdom
2022

Puttshack
Social entertainment focused
around mini-golf

Ascend Studio
ascendstudio.co.uk
United Kingdom / USA
2018

P

Prolet Property Services
Letting agency

JB Studio
jordanblyth.com
United Kingdom
2013

Quixel
Software tools for digital CG artists

1910 Design & Communication
weare1910.com
Sweden
2013

Quixit
App to turn digital pictures
from the mobile phone to real,
high quality, 10x10cm pictures

Bräutigam & Rotermund
braeutigam-rotermund.de
Germany
2013

Q

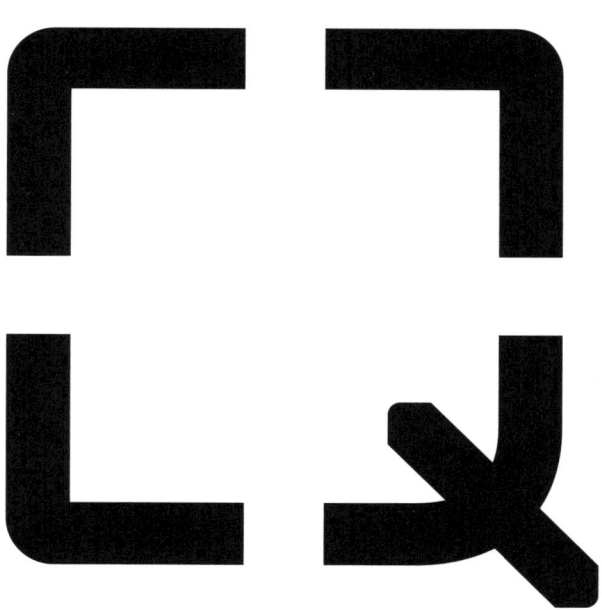

RESQWATER
Anti-hangover drink

Fellow
fellowinc.com
USA
2011

Q-Yacht
Services for yachts

Artiva Design
artiva.it
Italy
2007

Alterea Cogedim
Real estate company

Royalties
royalties.fr
France
2014

Quartermania Records
Record label

Sichtvermerk
sichtvermerk.com
Germany
2004

Q

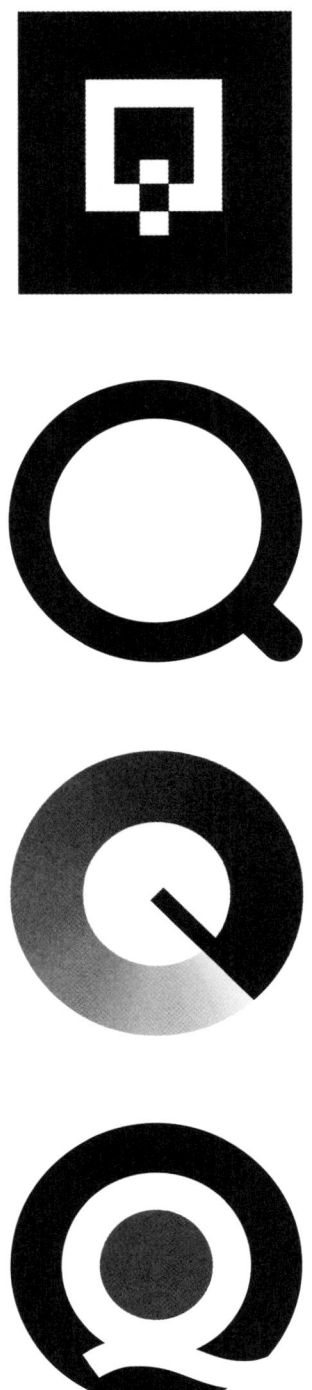

VCU Qatar Support Office
Liaison between the Richmond
& Qatar campuses of Virginia
Commonwealth University

eggnerd
eggnerd.com
USA
2008

Queens Museum of Art
Contemporary art museum

Q

Studio Lin
studiolin.org
USA
2010

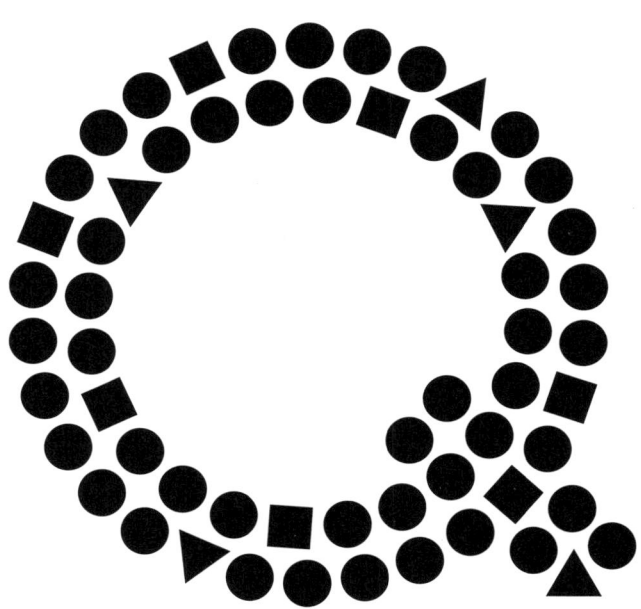

Quiet New World
Water therapy products

Leynivopnid
leynivopnid.is
Iceland
2013

Quality Foodcare
Food for patients in hospital

atelierworks.co.uk
Atelier Works
1994

Quik Chek
Retail

Lippincott
lippincott.com
USA
2008

Q

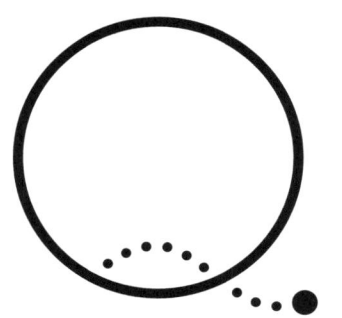

Qoin for 1Debit
Rewards program

Jonathan Patterson
jonathanpatterson.com
2013

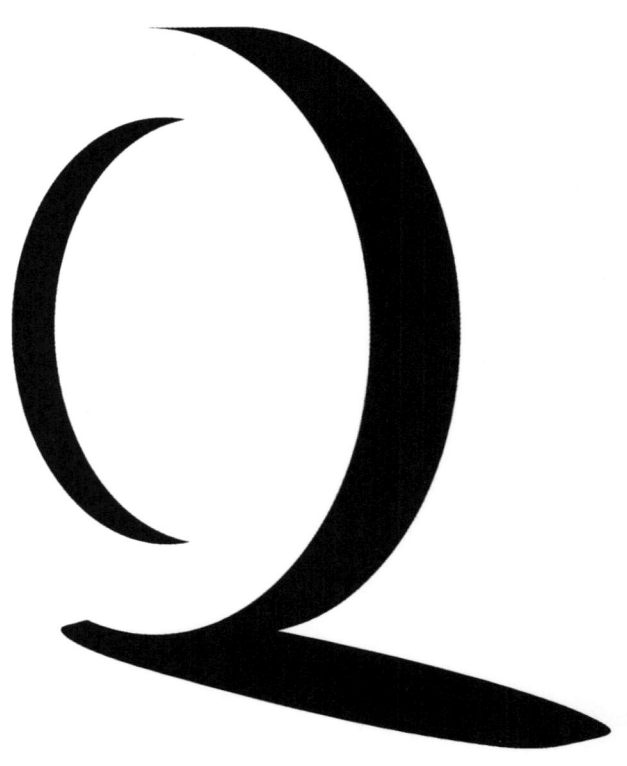

Rufflo Business Law
Business law for start-ups

Gee + Chung Design
geechungdesign.com
USA
2012

Ruby Blue
Liqueur

Rob Clarke Type Design & Lettering
robclarke.com
United Kingdom
2011

18 Rabbits
Granola company

Strohl
strohlsf.com
USA
2014

Radar (Registry of Advanced Diabetic Retinopathy)
Medical research

Parallax Design
parallaxdesign.com.au
Australia
2014

Roof.fm
Radio station

Fabian Leuenberger
fabianleuenberger.com
Switzerland
2008

Reichmann Ankvarier
Building antiquarian

Add Studio
addstudio.se
Sweden
2016

Raj Utracony (Paradise Lost)
Restaurant

Dmowski&Co.
dmowski.co
Poland
2022

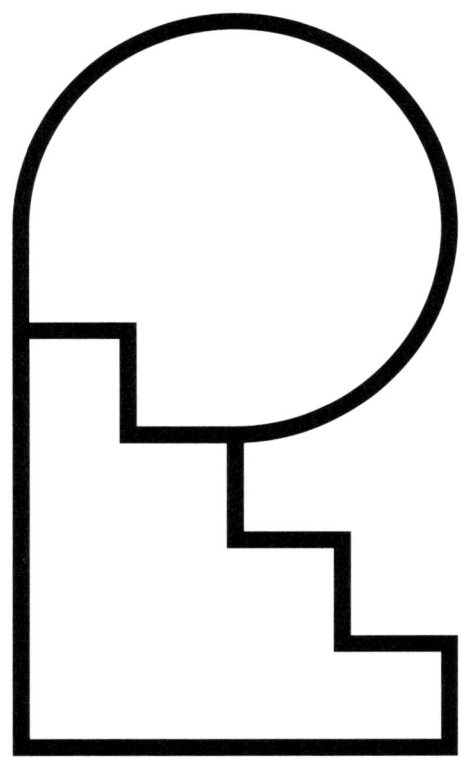

Ringle
Boat builder

Maud
maud.com.au
Australia
2012

Ryeberg
Website publishing essays about
online videos, curated by writers
& artists

Monnet Design
monnet.ca
Canada
2009

Rinse
Radio station, record label,
entertainment & events

Give Up Art
giveupart.com
United Kingdom
2006

Brands Republica
Concept store

Rafa Goicoechea / Small
rafagoicoechea.info
wearesmall.es
Spain
2013

R

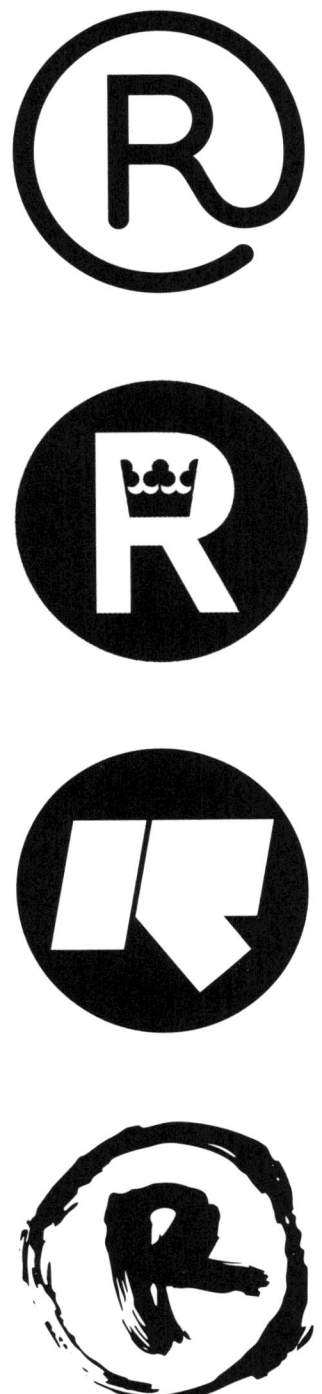

Resa
Recycled paper

Garbett Design
garbett.com.au
Australia
2008

Resolute
Print procurement

Mytton Williams
myttonwilliams.co.uk
United Kingdom
2004

Rob Clarke Type Design & Lettering
Self-initiated

Rob Clarke Type Design & Lettering
robclarke.com
United Kingdom
2010

Ruta del Vino y Brandy of Jerez
Association of wines from Jerez

Ángel Plaza
angel-plaza.com
Spain
2013

R

Regatta for Kustavin Puu Oy
Furniture manufacturer

Hahmo Design Oy
hahmo.fi
Finland
2008

REY
Social platform for tokenised assets

BRNVD®
brvnd.com
Dubai
2022

Refresher.sk
Lifestyle portal

Miro Kozel
mikodesign.sk
Slovakia
2013

R

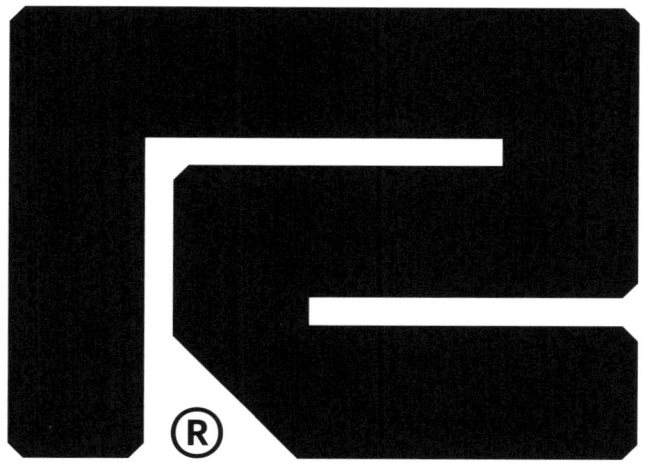

Rabbit
An independent coffee shop

The Click
theclickdesign.com
United Kingdom
2018

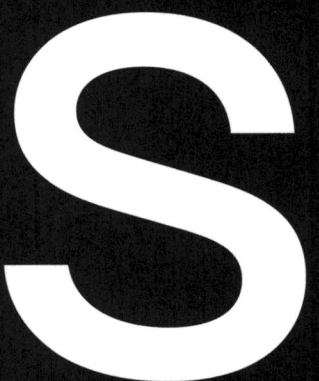

Scrimshaw Bar
Seafood bar

Ateljé Altmann
ateljealtmann.com
Sweden
2011

University of Art & Design
Helsinki University

Kari Piippo
piippo.com/kari
Finland
1991

The Swan Hotel
Hotel

Gareth Procter Studio
garethprocter.co.uk
United Kingdom
2012

s

Southernhay Chambers
Chambers of barristers

Believe in®
believein.co.uk
United Kingdom
2012

Nina Slavcheva
Photography

Atelier Dyakova
atelierdyakova.com
France
2018

Sonesta International Hotels
International chain of hotels

Malcolm Grear Designers
mgrear.com
USA
1979

Sophy Ltd
Manufacturer of hardwood
furniture products

Studio GT&P
tobanelli.com
Vietnam

Stampa
Limited edition prints

Studio Lin
studiolin.org
USA
2012

S

Sedgeford Sounds
Music production

Mash Creative
mashcreative.co.uk
USA
2013

Shanghoon
Photographer

Underline Studio
underlinestudio.com
Canada
2009

S

Our Studio
Architectural visualisation

eNaR
studioenar.co.uk
United Kingdom
2022

Sesamo
Restaurant located in a cave

Cruz Novillo
cruznovillo.com
Spain
1982

Special Fork
Recipe app

Brick Design
bricksf.com
USA
2010

Sliptraders
Moorage company

dng studio
dngstudio.com
Canada
2009

Storformat
Digital poster museum

Ateljé Altmann
ateljealtmann.com
Sweden
2010

Super Rugby for SANZAR (South African, New Zealand & Australian Rugby)
International rugby tournaments in the southern hemisphere

Moffitt.Moffitt.
moffittmoffitt.com
Australia / New Zealand / South Africa
2010

S

The Spectator Hotel
Hospitality

Stitch Design Co.
stitchdesignco.com
USA
2014

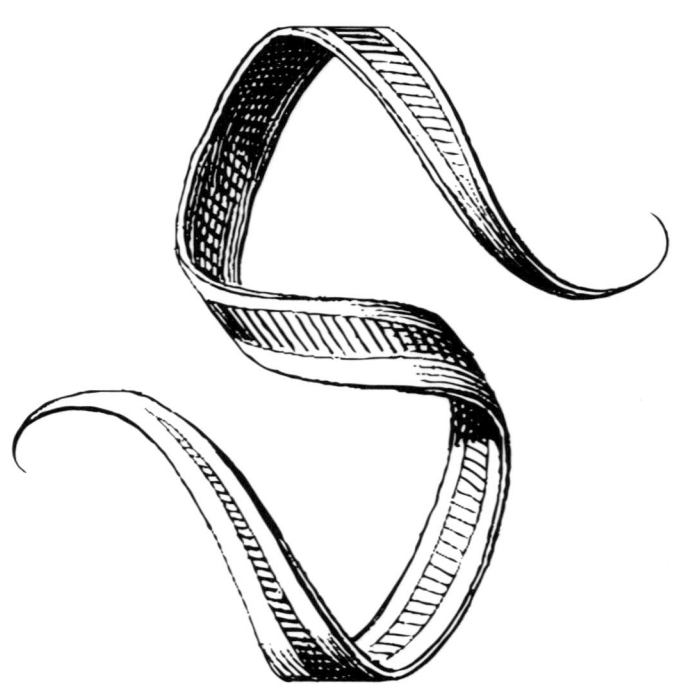

Casa Nostra
Italian seafood restaurant

Kobe Design Center Inc.
hatto-graphico.com
Japan
2008

Stewart Brewing
Brewery

O Street
ostreet.co.uk
United Kingdom
2020

Scarves Daily
Digitally printed scarf retailer

Kyle LaMar
kylelamar.com
USA
2012

Stone Supply
Distributor of natural stone

Chilli
Chilli.be
Belgium
2022

S

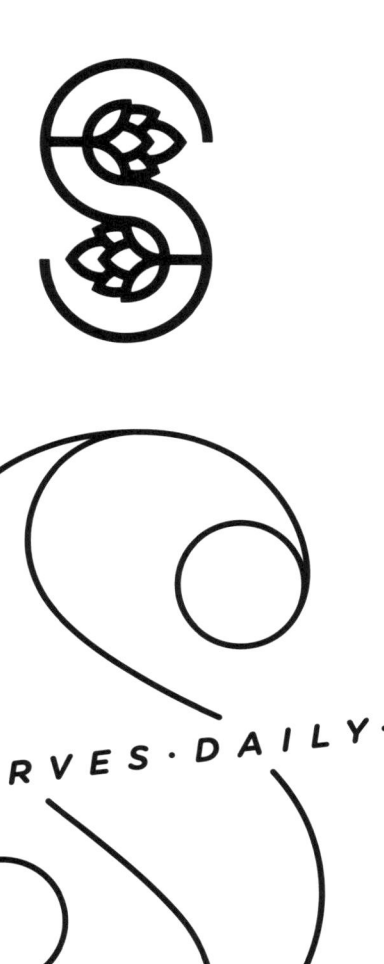

.SCARVES·DAILY·

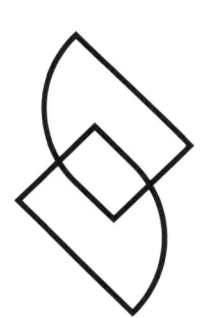

Stand mtl
Graphic design & strategy

Pointbarre
pointbarre.ca
Canada
2013

Stockton Propellers
Luxury motor yachts

Mash Creative
mashcreative.co.uk
United Kingdom
2007

Safnarad / The Museum Council of Iceland
Museum council

Leynivopnid
leynivopnid.is
Iceland
2013

Sunbelts
Manufacturer of leather accessories

Evers + de Gier
eversendegier.nl
Netherlands
2014

S

Siwar
Business

Foundry Collective
foundryco.com
Saudi Arabia
2013

Surus
Online store portal

Give Up Art
giveupart.com
United Kingdom
2009

Switch Communications, LLC.
Business communications

Studio Camo
studiocamo.com
USA
2014

Sisters
Shop selling healthy goods,
owned by two sisters

Leynivopnid
leynivopnid.is
Iceland
2013

S

Diputacion Provincial de Sevilla
DPS political administration

Cruz Novillo
cruznovillo.com
Spain
1993

StatSig
SaaS

Studio Mast
studiomast.co
USA
2023

Stygar
Digital media company

Mash Creative
mashcreative.co.uk
Austria
2009

Stock
Audiovisual production company

Cruz Novillo
cruznovillo.com
Spain
1984

S

Salomon
Mountain sport equipment & apparel

Planning Unit
planningunit.co.uk
France
2012

Songtrust
Music publishing

Order
order.design
USA
2021

Stonehaven
Lifetime mortgage servicer

Magpie Studio
magpie-studio.com
United Kingdom
2014

Studio Smith
Interior design consultancy

Mike Scott / MGS
mike-scott.co.uk
United Kingdom
2014

S

Sustainability Queensland
Sustainability services

inkahoots
inkahoots.com.au
Australia
2013

Sporveien
Public transport

Mission AS
mission.no
Norway
2021

Silverback
Specialist employment agency

Aad
studioaad.com
Ireland
2012

Freysmiles Orthodontics
Orthodontics

Nancy Wu Design
nancywudesign.com
USA
2010

S

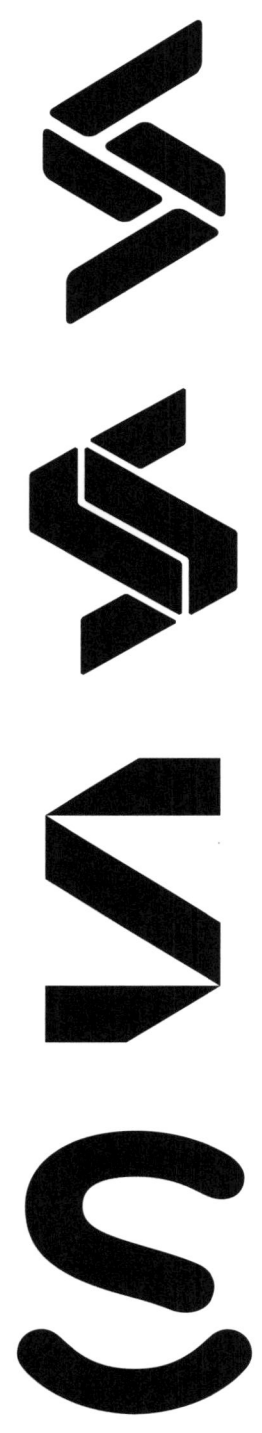

Smith Service Company
HVAC installation & service

The Hideout
thehideout.design
USA
2019

Symbol S
Furniture company

High Tide
hightidenyc.com
USA
2021

Seidre Lab
Web3 development

Mubien Brands
mubien.com
Australia
2022

Szic
Car dealer

Dmowski&Co.
dmowski.co
Poland
2021

The Sans
A refurbished modernist office building

Campbell Hay
campbellhay.com
United Kingdom
2022

Skarsgard Construction
Construction company

3 Advertising
3advertising.com
USA
2013

T

Torpedo, Oslo
Art & artist book store

Ariane Spanier Design
arianespanier.com
Norway
2006

Tequila
Nightclub

Bienal Comunicación
bienal.mx
Mexico
2014

Sali Tabacchi
Graphic design studio

Sali Tabacchi Inc.
salitabacchi.com
Canada
2007

Transproekt
Sofia

Stefan Kanchev
stefankanchev.com
Bulgaria
1950–1980

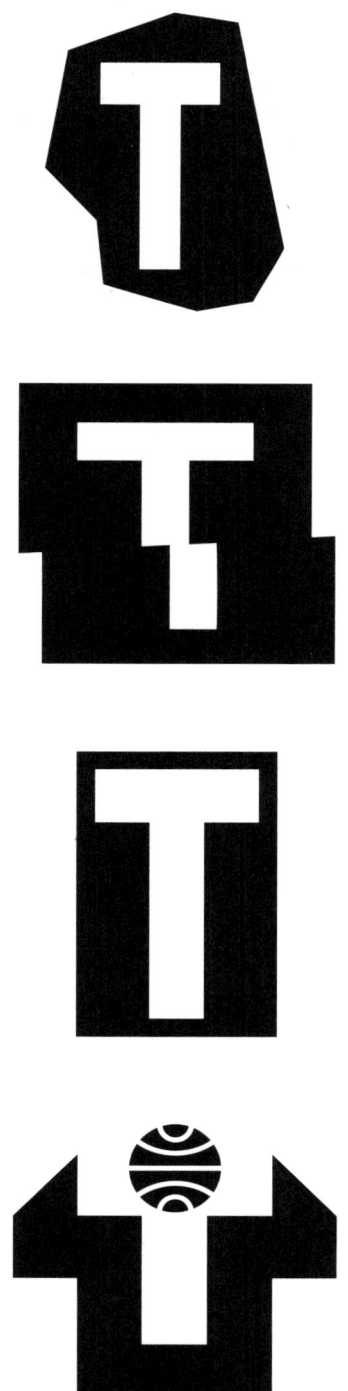

T

Teknologirådet
The Norwegian board of technology

Commando Group
commandogroup.no
Norway
2013

Tucker Gallery and Salon
Art gallery

Essex Two
sx2.com
USA
2011

Tabáres
Realty & building company

diseñollosa
diseñollosa.com.ar
Uruguay
1988

Triennale di Milano
International cultural institution

Italo Lupi
italolupistudio.com
Italy
1983

T

401

Trevi for Ideal Standard
Shower brand for bathroom
fittings manufacturer

Pentagram
pentagram.com
United Kingdom
Early 1990s

Tehnika Sofia
Publishing house

Stefan Kanchev
stefankanchev.com
Bulgaria
1950–1980

Terralec
Sound & lighting retailers

John Barton
johnbarton.co.uk
United Kingdom
2012

T

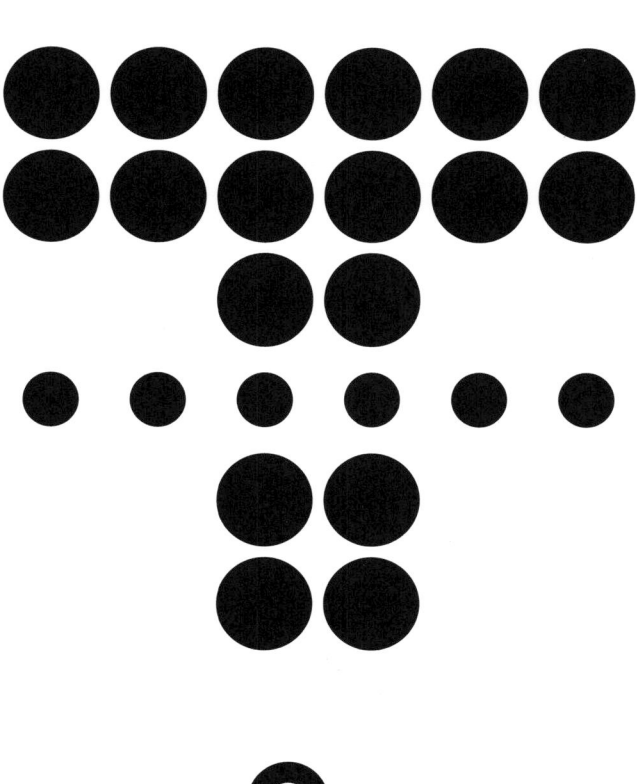

403

The Tree House
Housing developments

Mash Creative
mashcreative.co.uk
Canada
2014

Taskers
Workforce solutions & recruitment

Boy Bastiaens
stormhand.com
Netherlands
2011

Pencils Tehnikum
Technical school

Stefan Kanchev
stefankanchev.com
Bulgaria
1950–1980

Tabacalera de España
Manufacturing & distribution
of tobacco products

Malcolm Grear Designers
mgrear.com
Spain
2001

Teiman Filmes
Films

Pedro Paulino
pedropaulino.com
Brazil
2014

Twins Foundation
Membership organisation
and primary research center
on twins & other multiples

Malcolm Grear Designers
mgrear.com
USA
1983

Tracktivity
Motor racing app

Freytag Anderson
freytaganderson.com
USA
2014

Tabaqueira
Tobacco company

Miguel Palmeiro Designer
miguelpalmeiro.com
Portugal
2010

T

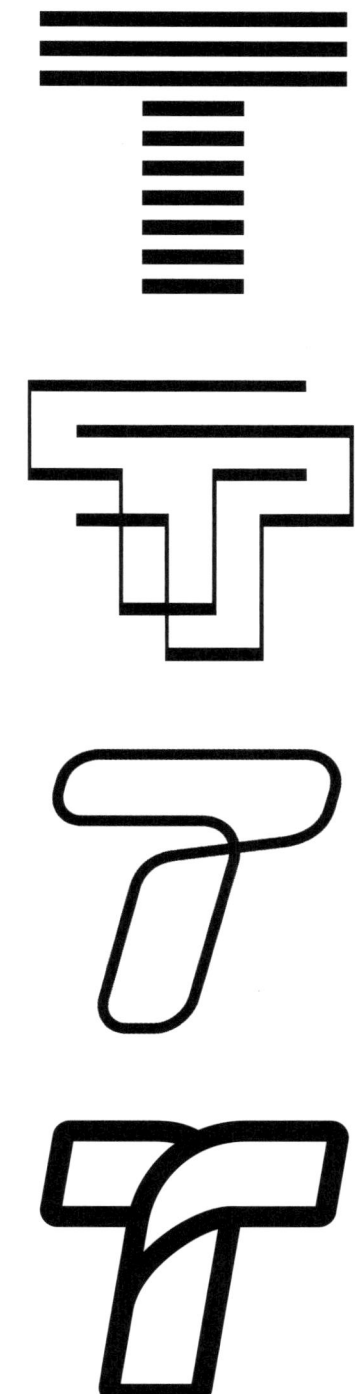

Twine
Online dating

SocioDesign
sociodesign.co.uk
United Kingdom
2013

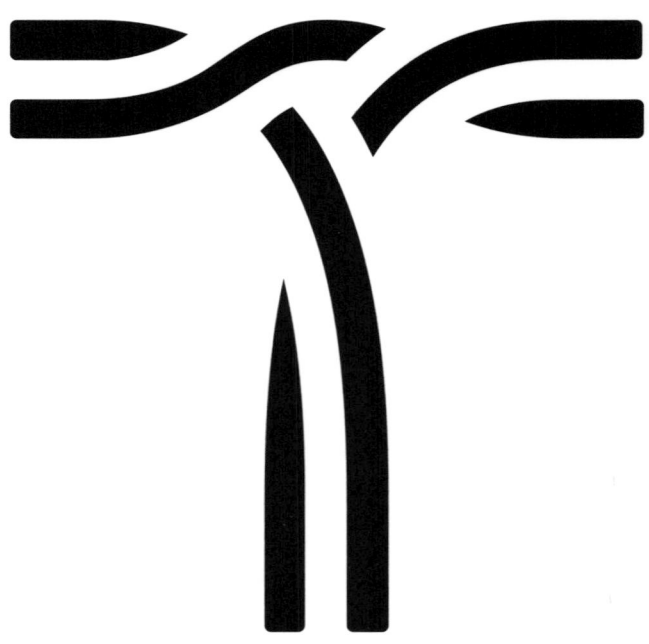

Turn
Phone app

Mash Creative
mashcreative.co.uk
United Kingdom
2012

TelePlace
Globally linked internet data centres

Gee + Chung Design
geechungdesign.com
USA
1999

Tokenology Labs
NFT cryptopedia

Mubien Brands
mubien.com
USA
2022

Tavelwerket
Online posters

Add Studio
addstudio.se
Sweden
2018

TAKK
Coffee house

Studio DBD
studiodbd.com
United Kingdom
2013

T

GoTrendier
Second hand selling & buying app

Mariela Mezquita
marielamezquita.com
Mexico
2017

Think Thorne
Office design & interior solutions

Distil Studio
distilstudio.co.uk
United Kingdom
2013

Technical City Engineering Ltd.
Construction industry

for&st
for-st.co
Hong Kong, China
2022

Tropic
Bioscience

Koto
koto.studio
United Kingdom
2021

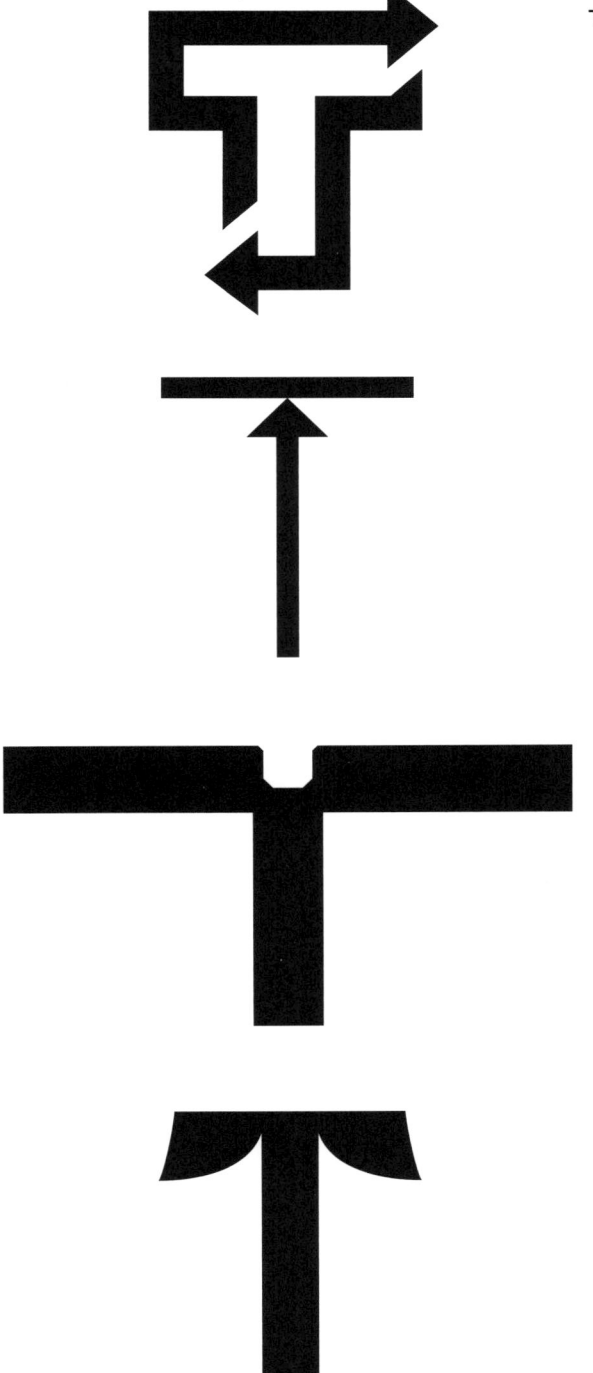

T

The Tailor
Travel agent

Parallax Design
parallaxdesign.com.au
Australia
2011

Triennale di Milano
International cultural institution

Italo Lupi
italolupistudio.com
Italy
1983

Talsa for Grupo Rocío
Brand of agricultural exporter

Brandlab
brandlab.pe
Peru
2013

t.lovers
Serving high quality tea

Bräutigam & Rotermund
braeutigam-rotermund.de
Germany
2013

T

415

Tunnel
Disco

Milani Design
milanidesign.it
USA
1986

UrbanSpaces
Commercial interior design

dng studio
dngstudio.com
Canada
2010

The Ultimate Sausage
Snack food

U

Rob Clarke Type Design & Lettering /
Elmwood
robclarke.com
United Kingdom
2010

Ulysses
Theater performances

Essex Two
sx2.com
USA
1994

Ulster University
University

AVB Brand
avb-brand.com
United Kingdom
2014

Union Yard
Independent tea & coffee shop

The Click
theclickdesign.com
United Kingdom
2012

U

FOOD4U
Event catering service

JB Studio
jordanblyth.com
United Kingdom
2012

uBear
Mobile phone & computer accessories

Mash Creative / Hype Type Studio
mashcreative.co.uk
hypetype.co.uk
USA
2014

Ultramar
Hotel, nature resort & spa

Aitor Baigorri
aitorbaigorri.com
Spain
2019

Ultratkt
Barcode solutions company

Duane Dalton
duanedalton.com
USA
2013

Üla
Graphic design & illustration

üla
ula.com.ar
Argentina
2020

U

Unistream
Money transfer service

Maksim Arbuzov
maksimarbuzov.com
Russia
2011

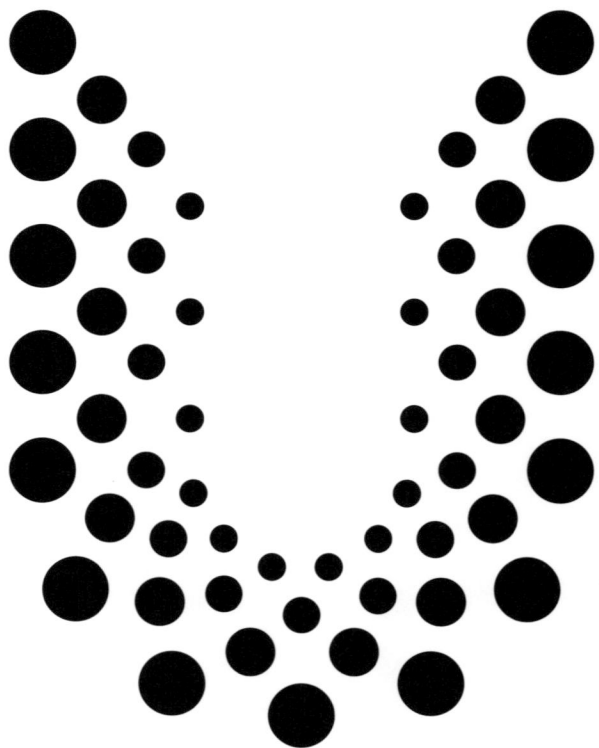

The Vitamin Shoppe
Retail

Lippincott
lippincott.com
USA
2013

Vale
Mining

Lippincott
lippincott.com
Brazil
2007

CV Photography
Photography

Mash Creative
mashcreative.co.uk
USA
2013

Vehicle
Record label

Give Up Art
giveupart.com
United Kingdom
2001

V

Vanderbilt University
University

Malcolm Grear Designers
mgrear.com
USA
2001

Vivité
Online health document offering
access to medical histories

Thomas Manss & Company
manss.com
Germany
2011

Vivense London
Furniture & decor retailer

BOB Design
bobdesign.co.uk
United Kingdom
2020

Visant
Marketing & publishing

Lippincott
lippincott.com
USA
2005

v

431

Veristream
Security technologies & visitor management systems

Büro Ink
bueroink.com
USA
2007

Wyzwolenie
Night club

Dmowski & Co.
dmowski.co
Poland
2014

Alexandria Wall
Artist management

Travis Ladue
travisladue.com
USA
2013

Wisconsin Power Company
Electricity provider

Essex Two
sx2.com
USA
1993

Wheatsheaf
Investors in businesses that develop
sustainable food & energy initiatives

Telling Stories
tellingstories.co.uk
United Kingdom
2013

w

Wandering Cooks
Kitchens & community for food entrepreneurs

inkahoots
inkahoots.com.au
Australia
2012

w

Wriggly Tin
F&B

Studio Mast
studiomast.co
USA
2023

Windstream
Telecommunications

Lippincott
lippincott.com
USA
2006

W Solutions
Technical insulation systems

DM Workroom Ltd
dmworkroom.com
France
2013

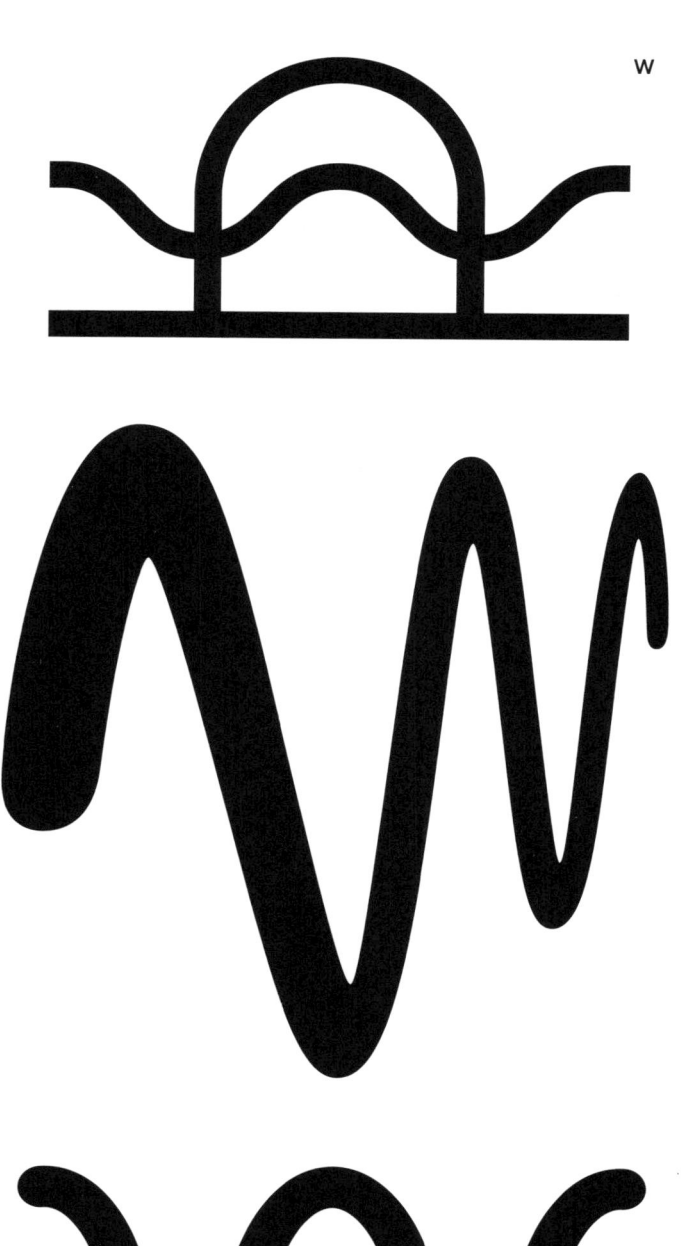

WARC
Online service offering advertising
best practice, evidence & insights
from the world's leading brands

Studio David Hillman
studiodavidhillman.com
United Kingdom
2008

w

Weev
Social video

d.studio
d-studio.co.uk
USA
2014

Winters Design & Build
Designer & builder of houses

Sali Tabacchi Inc.
salitabacchi.com
Canada
2012

Professor Dr. med. Kurt Götz Wurster
Specialist in gynecology & sports medicine

stapelberg&fritz
stapelbergundfritz.com
Germany
2007

Wealth Horizon
Financial services

Mytton Williams
myttonwilliams.co.uk
United Kingdom
2014

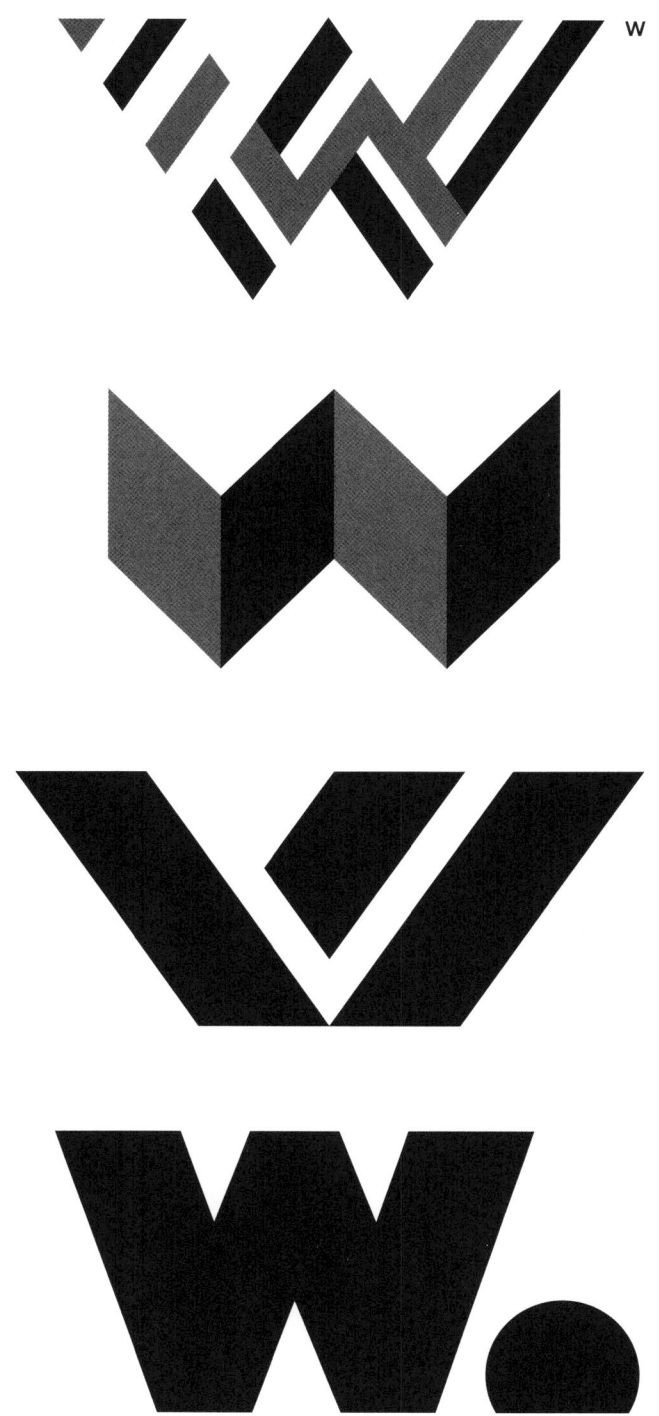

Walnut Consulting
Management consultants

I See Sea
iseesea.co.uk
United Kingdom
2010

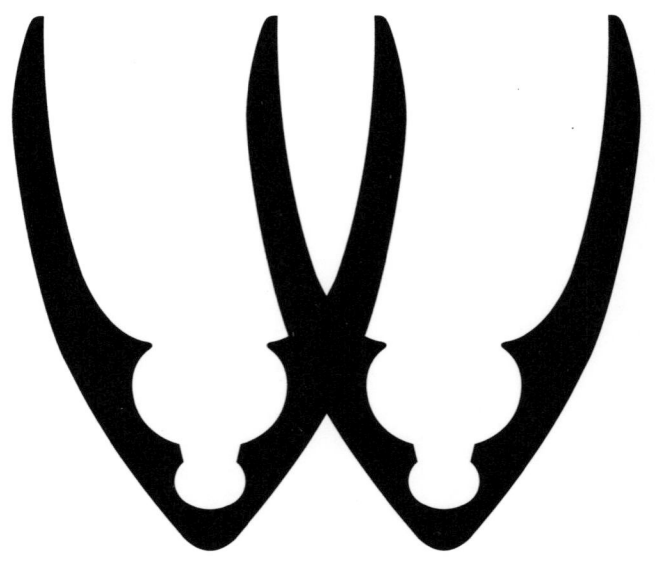

The Wood Rack
Full service design-build
remodeling contractors

Group T Design
grouptdesign.com
USA
2003

Dublin Writers Festival
Arts festival

Aad
studioaad.com
Ireland
2011

Widening
Startup accelerator

Artiva Design
artiva.it
USA
2014

Artvvork
Inspiration blog

Face
designbyface.com
Mexico
2011

Westboro Nursery School
Childcare & education

idApostle
idapostle.com
Canada
2009

w

Webtech Wireless
GPS fleet tracking

Nancy Wu Design
nancywudesign.com
Canada
2010

Wijngoed Rhode
Wine

Chilli
chilli.be
Belgium
2014

Wixx
Telecom

BRBAUEN
brbauen.com
Brazil
2018

w

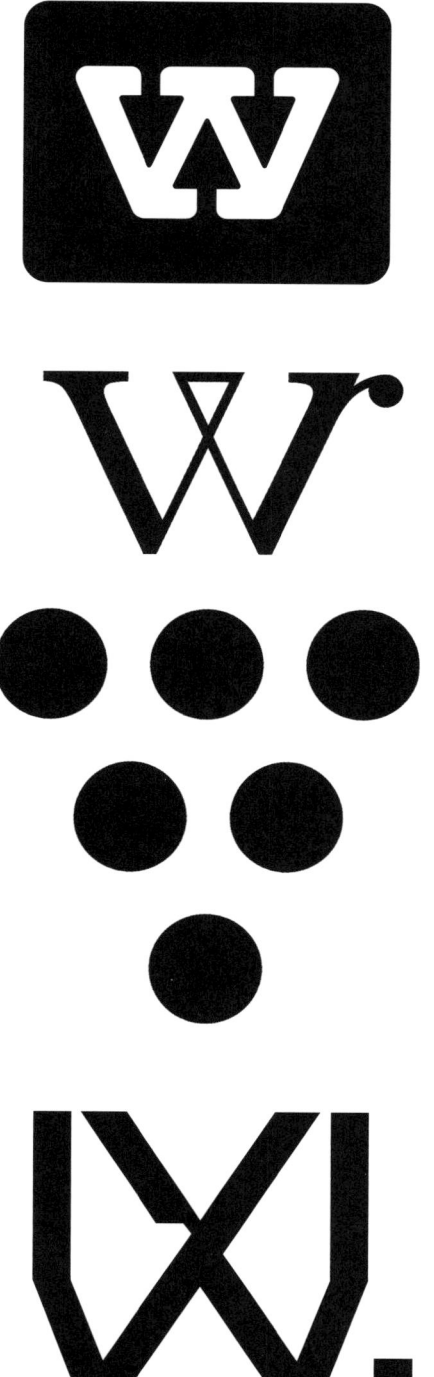

449

Wedding Ring Shop
Jewellery store

Wall-to-Wall Studios
walltowall.com
USA
2011

Window Film Company
Vinyl graphics

SocioDesign
sociodesign.co.uk
United Kingdom
2012

NBCUniversal
Global media & entertainment company

Wolff Olins
wolffolins.com
USA
2010

Wiredscore
Property technology firm

SomeOne
someoneinlondon.com
United Kingdom
2020

W

Wednesday's Domaine
Alcohol-free wine

Alec Tear
alectear.com
United Kingdom
2022

Xersion
Retail

Fellow
fellowinc.com
USA
2013

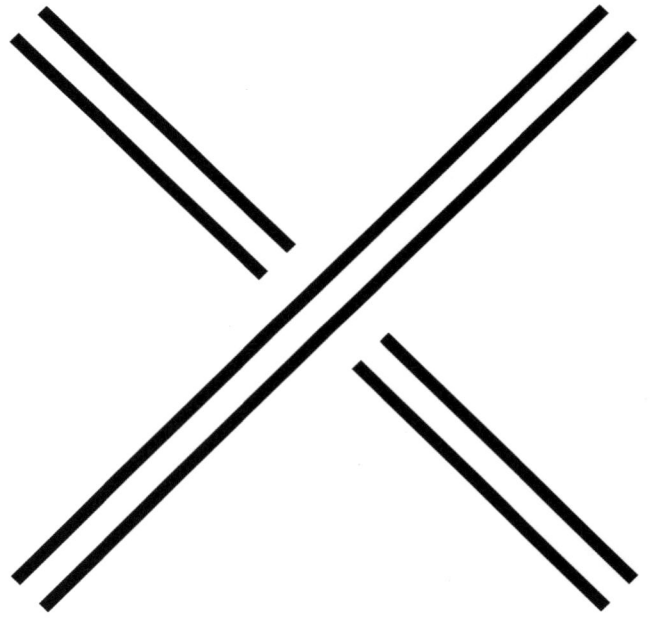

YONEKURA MFG
Industrial measuring & test
equipment manufacturer

Common graphic
common-graphic.com
Japan
2007

XYZ

Yellow Jacket
Health & safety management software

Rob Clarke Type Design & Lettering / 400
robclarke.com
United Kingdom
2011

Zoombis
Print-on-demand company

Wall-to-Wall Studios
walltowall.com
USA
2008

YU
Fashion

Canefantasma
canefantasma.com
United Kingdom
2018

Yeah! Indie Club
Music club

Quim Marin
quimmarin.com
Spain
2013

XYZ

YMCA
Non-profit community organisation

Siegel+Gale
siegelgale.com
United Kingdom
2011

Art On You
Creative space for workshops

Marisa Piñana
marisapinana.com
Spain
2019

Yellowatt
Solar energy

Studio Echt
studioecht.com
Slovakia
2023

Zirx
Parking

Brandclay
brandclay.com
USA
2014

LayerZ
Music venue

Canefantasma
canefantasma.com
United Kingdom
2018

Banco Zaragozano
Bank

Cruz Novillo
cruznovillo.com
Spain
1989

Zamorano
Hairdresser

Cruz Novillo
cruznovillo.com
Spain
1970

XYZ

461

Zerowatt
Household appliances

Milani Design
milanidesign.it
Italy
1978

Farmazia Zumárraga
Pharmacy

Lucas Gil Turner Branding & Design
lucasgilturner.com
Spain
2013

Zonik
Retail

Lippincott
lippincott.com
Saudi Arabia
2007

Z.Ballerini
Designer & retailer

moodley brand identity
moodley.at
USA
2013